LUCIFER ZENITH

CORRUPTING NATURE'S GOD
THROUGH GOVERNMENT DECEPTION

DANIEL R. MERCURI

CONTENTS

DEDICATION

This book is dedicated to my family.

To my beautiful oldest daughter, you are the absolute apple of my eye. I adore your marvelous high-spirited glee. I will exhaust myself if only to give you a brighter future for a life filled with love and great joy. At the writing of this book, you are battling leukemia. Every day has become a fight we are facing together as a family, but it is your perseverance that encourages me to continue to fight the good fight to protect your future. I pray daily Jesus keeps his healing hands upon you.

To my amazing son, you will forever be my pride and joy. You have a comedian's talent, always aiming to make your family laugh. You wear your beautiful heart on your sleeve. I am steadfast on making sure you live in a world that respects honorable men just like the man that I see you are becoming.

To my adorable and youngest daughter, you have added a new level of happiness I didn't think was possible to my life. You are your mother's mini-me and will forever be my bundle of joy. I can only hope one day you can look back and know that your father fought to make sure you would never have to endure these strange and tumultuous days that we are living in now.

To my wife, there's an old adage, *behind every good man there is a great woman,* is an understatement when it comes to all that you have endured. You love hard and fight hard. Your wonderful gentleness has inspired my bravery, your sweet innocence has calmed my spirit, your vigor has encouraged my dutifulness, your honesty has strengthened my courage, your support has harnessed my devotion to our marriage, and your faith in Christ Jesus emboldens my belief. You have championed all that I have set out to accomplish even when I stand in the face of affliction. It is by your council that I have embarked into the writing of this book. It is by your love that I am determined to…sound the alarm.

PREFACE

Since I have ventured into the writing of this book, I will have spent nearly five years campaigning for political office and it will be a total of seven years by the completion of the 2026 election cycle. I have been desperately trying to figure out the reasoning behind why the People's grievances are falling on willful and complicit representative deaf ears. This book is a culmination of my experiences and focused research on this subject matter. It is a piecing together and simplification of the complex web designed to keep the People under the weight of government and how it ties into biblical prophecies. This book will either leave you in anger, disbelief, or frustration. You may even be compelled to dismiss it in hopes to remain blissfully ignorant. Take the information for what it's worth and remember to test the spirit of the information just as iron sharpens iron before you believe in anything.

INTRODUCTION

People have asked me on numerous occasions throughout my gubernatorial campaigns in California, "Daniel, why do you want to try and attempt to become the governor? You're taking on Goliath." I always responded, "No, I'm not taking on Goliath. I'm taking on Goliath and his four brothers, but my name is Daniel and I'm very used to being in the lion's den."

My journey in campaigning for political office began in 2019, when I ran for a congressional seat in California's 25th District Special Election. I decided to campaign for this position after finding out that former Congresswoman Katie Hill was vacating her seat before she publicly announced her resignation and my district was going to be left without representation. My only intention was to fill the void left for the People of my district.

I'd always known, as many Americans do that there are many levels of corruption operating behind the scenes within our government. It was during that congressional special election that I personally experienced how deep the widespread government villainy truly ran. I was exposed to the corporatists' deceitful contracts, the lobbyists' backend deals, the Super-Pac campaign donation bribery, as well as the GOP and DNC's joint collaboration in fundraising that is used to character assassinate candidates who fight against their desired narrative.

I didn't win that congressional seat, but I gained something more valuable. I learned how the political arena worked. I realized the most positive impact I could make for the People of my state and perhaps the entire country was in the seat of California Governor. There is a popular saying that *whatever happens in California, so goes the rest of the nation.* In my humble opinion, next to the Presidency, the seat of California Governor is the second highest coveted office in all of the land. If the People can set California right, then maybe the rest of the corruption will slowly become more impotent.

In April of 2020, following Governor Gavin Newsom's March Executive Order N67-20, the *Stay at Home Safe Order*, I began my 2022 gubernatorial journey. In 2021 Governor Gavin Newsom was being recalled and a special election took place to which my team and I worked vigorously to make the ballot. Unfortunately, Governor Gavin Newsom was not unseated. However, I remained resolute on continuing with my original goal to run in the 2022 gubernatorial primary election. Despite the momentum I had gained from the recall, it still wasn't enough for me to get the notoriety or funding I needed to outpace my opponents.

I knew I couldn't just let all the experience and knowledge I had obtained up to this point go by the wayside. During my campaigns, I inadvertently became a constitutionalist. That title of a constitutionalist came to me by way of the People. Many hosts from the radio shows, podcasts, forums, and the debates I was invited to, began to dub me as "the only Constitutional Candidate" or "Constitutionalist and Candidate, Daniel Mercuri." I was extremely humbled by an incredible and very intelligent man Mr. Constitutionalist himself, Douglas V. Gibbs, during the 2022 gubernatorial race who rated me based on my constitutional understanding as the only five-star candidate out of all the gubernatorial candidates that year.

Now I'm on a four-year journey to educate the People on all I have learned prior to returning to the campaign front in 2026 for California Governor. I want to remind them that the Framers of this great experiment they called the United States of America established a republic form of government not a democracy. The word democracy was repugnant to our Forefathers. They knew power must reside in the hands of the People. The People of today need to focus and start utilizing their power to stop fighting for civil rights and start fighting to maintain what's left of their unalienable rights that are endowed to them by the Creator which is so heavily protected in the United States for America's Constitution. Civil rights and unalienable rights have never been one in the same and are not interchangeable. We the People of the United States of America need to re-involve ourselves passionately back into politics instead of passively handing off the responsibility to our elected representatives who continue to draft and vote in egregious legislation that attempts to strip us of our natural, God-given rights. All too often we refuse to interrupt our decadent lives for fear of retaliation and as a result it is costing us all of our freedoms.

We need to relearn that it is the sovereign that can prevent unconstitutional laws from operating falsely under the color of law. This can only be achieved through knowing the U.S. Constitution and your state constitution(s). As a nation we have forgotten that it is the consent of the governed who grant authoritative powers to their elected representatives. The state of corruption in our government is perpetuated by the ignorant people who continue to vote back in the degenerates that have already proven they've turned their backs on their own constituents during previous terms of service.

Too many people have become automatons when it comes to voting for a favored candidate. Rather than doing their own investigation and analysis into each and every candidate, they wait for their party like the GOP, DNC, or mainstream media to send out their candidate selects on who the People should choose. Instead of focusing on the candidates constitutional understanding, voters focus on how much money the candidate has amassed for their campaigns. Comparatively, voters fail to focus on the nature and character of the candidate. Instead, they center on electability which is based on popularity in addition to a candidate's ability to raise funds. They mourn for principled representation, but re-elect career politicians who pander to the highest bidder. They seek new leadership rather than new servants. They scream for political rights in place of unalienable endowments. If the voters only knew how infiltrated each of those groups had become, they might just become their own agents of truth and would easily identify candidates with moral decree instead of falling prey to concubine lip service. The need to clean house and remove the career swindlers out of office was a key point I would express to the people I met while campaigning. Unless the American people become more educated, they will never be able to simply vote out these rogue politicians.

As a gubernatorial political candidate, I became privy to a lot of the hardships every county was enduring within my state of California. Republicans, Democrats, Independents, Non-Partisans etc. were all talking about the need for greater transparency and accountability in order to start addressing the problems. However, no group or candidate really wanted to define what that transparency meant or what that accountability looked like. Often candidates come to a belief that they must pander systematically for fear of losing votes while they are campaigning. They believe that is how the game must be played. Let me first say, this is not a game to me. Second, let me be the first California gubernatorial candidate willing to define accountability. It means prison! When you violate your oath of office, it is no different than being a criminal. What do we do with criminals? They go to jail. That's accountability! Yet we have so many burgeoning wannabe representatives that tell their potential constituents that they're going to negotiate with the current status quo. Why? Negotiating new and egregious legislative Senate Bills (SB) or Assembly Bills (AB) with a criminal makes you a criminal.

Domestic enemies are still enemies whether they've been voted into office legally or they are a foreign nation attacking the United States from distant shores. Their desired outcome for the fall of our nation and the continued enslavement of our people is the same. I have no desire to bring any domestic enemy to the table. There is no table! They destroyed it with their deceit. They destroyed the Constitution by undermining its foundational framework. They destroyed our sovereignty for serfdom. They destroyed everything any military veteran fought honorably to protect and preserve. I do not negotiate with the perverse, the reprobates, the duplicitous, the pedophiles, and the evil vile who are turning on the very people they swore to protect. No one should ever be okay with their newly elected representative negotiating with the treasonous.

Many have said to me, "Daniel, I just can't get political." Well, do you like the price of gas that you're paying today? That's political. Do you like the educational system in California? At the writing of this book, California is ranked 44th in the nation.

That's political. Did you like it when the scammers told you during the Wuhan Virus/Covid-19 lockdowns that you couldn't go to church? That's political. How about when Governor Gavin Newsom told Californians that they could go back to church, but they just couldn't sing? That was political. How about the utility companies in California now charging people for electricity based off of personal income? That's political. Everything is political. Your paycheck, property taxes, food, and the road management are political. It's ALL political. If you simply cannot get political, then you must acknowledge that you are part of the problem because you are part of perpetuating the very cycle of oppression you complain about instead of becoming a part of the solution.

CHAPTER 1

THE MIND OF DANIEL

I want people to understand that the information I am presenting in this book did not come easily to me. There was a deep part of me that needed to understand the big WHY behind HOW there could be so much widespread government deception. I had finally reached a point where I no longer wanted to be bewildered by the on-going authority extortion and allow myself to be blissfully ignorant. I wanted truth no matter how hard it was going to be to face. I had to learn how to see through the lies hidden in the complex propaganda. I know many people have woken up, but they are still struggling through the self-education process. They are desperately trying to figure out how we got into this mess in the first place and learn what we can do to fight back. I truly believe the only way we're going to end the dissension of government depravity is through education. I have been educating myself through research and seeking answers for the last five years. I want to help people get to the answers quicker. I believe if you understand more about my educational struggles and background, you will understand that I am just an ordinary, common person looking for the solutions to push back against the gaslighting that is so heavily plaguing our lives. I hope this will encourage you not to give up on finding your own answers, to be a critical thinker, an active investigator, and know that all it takes is diligence.

When I was in the military I struggled academically because I had grown up with poor study habits. I was a 'C' student all through my elementary, junior high, and high school years. I'm not proud of that and it wasn't for a lack of trying. It was because I didn't quite understand how my mind worked.

Several years after high school, I joined the United States Navy and set on a path to becoming a Search and Rescue (SAR) Aircrewman Rescue Swimmer. The physical trials and training were easy. I had been an athlete since I was a child, but academics were my Achilles heel. I was forced to spend long, hard, and arduous hours going over material during my training because most of the material I was required to learn was classified, secret, or top secret. I couldn't just take it home. I had to leave the material in guarded vaults. Whenever it was possible for me to stay late and review priority subjects, I did. It was from that work ethic that I was fortunate to score first or second place in all of my classes and training. I don't know what it was like for other service members in other branches, but at the time I served in the Navy the top two sailors with the highest scores always got to choose their orders. So, I made it a point to get a score high enough to have that first or second pick.

One of my early barrack roommates, Mikey, just so happened to have a photographic memory. I never really believed people could have that capability until I met him. One late night, when studying the Naval Air Training and Operating Procedure Standards (NATOPS) manual, Mikey asked me what I was struggling with. I said, "I just can't commit all this material to memory."

He laughed and said something so profound that it has always stuck with me. He said, "You never learned how to learn."

It was like a lightbulb went on in my head. *Learn how to learn.* We never teach our children to *learn how to learn* first. We teach them a subject matter and expect them to grasp the material by repetition, but that doesn't always work for everyone. We need to first try and figure out how their brain uniquely works. What is it about the subject matter that they gravitate towards the most? That's what Mikey did with me. He sat down on that late evening and said, "Let's start with the NATOPS manual. What do you like about the aircraft?"

Of course, I hated the NATOPS manual. Most of the Aircrew candidates did because it was a dry, lengthy manual thicker than the Bible. I said, "I love to do the SAR jumps out of the helicopter."

He said, "Great! Let's look at the cabin door when we're flying in that aircraft and you open it up."

We started flipping backwards and forwards learning all the information about the aircraft cabin door. He then asked, "What else do you like?"

I said, "I'm a fan of dangling from underneath the helicopter from the rescue hook when being hoisted up after a swimmer jump."

Mikey replied, "Sweet! Let's look at the rescue hook. What

else?"

I said, "I love to shoot."

He enthusiastically responded with a, "F-- ya! Me too. So, let's look at all the connecting parts when attaching the M60, the M240, and the 50cal."

As the night continued on, Mikey and I started realizing I am a nonlinear learner. I have to find the subject areas within the subject, whether it's psychology, history, or philosophy that I gravitate towards and study from that point of the material first. Eventually, I will familiarize myself with all of the material quickly and efficiently. For the first time in my life while studying with Mikey, I could truly digest the information I was studying and I was able to commit the most important key topics to memory with ease.

Years later, I went to community college after I got out of the military. I applied the same learning process and was able to get A's, B's, and even made the Dean's list a few times. Learning had always been a challenge resulting in fruitless effort and now it had become simple for me because I had learned the right skills to learn how I learned best. I took that same methodology to try and figure out what we could do to hold these corrupt representatives responsible. How could we hold them liable? What could a governor really do to clean house, legally, lawfully, and according to the Constitution? I'm going to tell you right now, if you are unwilling to disrupt your lifestyle then you really don't want your freedoms because freedom involves sacrifice. Freedom involves the hard truths!

If you are a Christian, you probably have a Bible with notes written all over the margins and highlights up and down on virtually every page. Almost all Christians have at least one of those Bibles. Now answer this, have you ever read the United States Constitution in its entirety? How about the Declaration of Independence? Ever read the Magna Carta of 1215? Do you still study them to this day? Most people would say, no. Have you ever read your own state constitution? I have asked dozens, if not hundreds of people, if they've ever read their own California State Constitution? I would ask it to a room full of California GOP (CA GOP) or California Republican Assembly (CRA) members from different county caucuses and less than three people in a room of fifty to three hundred would raise their hands. I was stunned. I would shout, "Why not? This is your state. This should be chalked up like your Bible. This defines the limitation of powers granted to your state representatives which also has to be in agreement with the Supreme Law of the Land!"

If you don't know your state constitution or the United States Constitution, how can you address your representatives with redresses of grievances when you don't truly know if government representation has engaged in egregious acts?

To all of you who are now reading this book, it's imperative that you understand if you don't know your rights, you have no rights. If you don't know the law, there is no law.

Activism is wonderful because it brings awareness to the community, but holding up a sign over a freeway overpass will not change the hearts and minds of the morbidly corrupt.

Personally, I am done holding up signs on the corner of a street or standing in front of a building protesting my grievances to the complicit. It's time for everyone to engage in what's actionable. You have to engage in actionable processes that are going to get these bought and paid for officials out of office and into prison. It's not going to be easy. You most certainly won't hit a homerun your first time out or even the third time out. It's going to be time consuming and require day in and day out efforts. Let me remind everyone that there were six attempts to recall California Governor Gavin Newsom. It was the fifth attempt that succeeded, but there was actually a little known sixth filing that took place before the fifth attempt was publicly acknowledged to have been successful.

Many people in California have told me that they agree with my stance about cleaning house. They would say they're in full support of it. However, they always follow up their affirmation with a big question, "How are you going to clean house?" In order for me to tell you how as a governor these people could be held accountable and sent to prison, you have to first understand how the American people got into this mess in the first place. Allow me to take you on that journey.

CHAPTER 2

HOW TO SPEAK TREASON

Can the People fight corrupt government when everything is falling on deaf ears? The answer is, yes. We CAN win it back. In order for the People to fight back properly, they must first discern how to speak treason. You need to understand that the language of treason deals in double speak. Saying yes and no all at the same time. It involves confounding WHAT IS through language manipulation in order to create an illegal legislative loophole that appears lawful on the surface. This is a primary weapon of choice by all dictators. To summarize, in its most simplistic form, *the language of treason is when the corrupt in government change the language to change perception in order to pass repugnant legislation so that the morbidly twisted can engage in their continued perversions, contractually, and without remorse.*

When a state proposition is placed on a ballot and the People have to vote yes or no on that prop, often the People feel like when they voted yes, they really voted no and when they voted no, they really voted yes. This is ambiguity at its finest. Unfortunately, we are at the point where it doesn't matter if you vote yes or no on any proposition. If not done through affirmative action, the puppet masters through their legislations are going to get their way regardless of how you vote.

Let's review some examples. If we look back to 2022, California

State AB 2223 infamously known as the Infanticide Bill was drafted by Assemblywoman Buffy Wicks who removed the word phrasing *crimes against nature* and changed *pregnant woman* to *pregnant person*. This alone abrogates the Declaration of Independence which is the foundation to the Articles of Confederation. At best, a *person* is ambiguous to that which is of *Nature and of Nature's God*. Why? Because a woman by the *Laws of Nature* is female and nature only allows a woman or female creature to birth a child or offspring. The use of the word *person* when reading law, implies ambiguously any sex can birth a child or offspring. This is not biologically or anatomically possible. Assemblywoman Buffy Wicks deliberately changed the language to create an illegal loophole in order to undermine and subvert the U.S. Constitution and the California State Constitution. This was a major violation to her oath of office, a duty she swore to uphold.

Sadly, this bill passed which updated the California State Constitution egregiously in 2023 under Article I. Sec. 1.1. This act indefinitely permits abortions to be protected under the *Privacy Clause* of the California State Constitution. This is an exploitation of the last word *privacy* under Article I. Sec. 1. If abortions fall under *privacy*, then ALL things medically related must fall under privacy. This would include adult and childhood vaccinations or the lack thereof. Any public health order, mandate, regulation, or statute cannot operate outside constitutional rights. Those directives cannot turn a right into a privilege. Section 1.1 is also an abridgment to Article I. Sec. 1 of the California State Constitution. Pro-choice advocates would argue that the woman has a right to bodily autonomy when dealing with pregnancy. Unfortunately, that is incorrect. The right to bodily autonomy is also appropriated to the unborn child who falls under the *Laws of Nature and of*

Nature's God as written in the Declaration of Independence. A servant of the People has the primary function of defending their entitlements endowed by the Creator, the right to life being one of them. The unborn infant has a right to life especially during its natural course of gestation. How else does one secure the blessings to their posterity if government allows for purposeful disruption against the acts of one's provenience?

Another example is found from California in 2022 when legislators passed AB1149. This bill allowed a 12-year-old's medical record to no longer be accessible to parents because the bill redefined *parents* as *representatives*. Remember, everything falls back to the Declaration of Independence under *Nature and of Nature's God*, meaning *Common Law*. Parents fall within the *Laws of Nature* when it comes to parental rights and their child's upbringing. Parents, not government, are there by the *Laws of Nature* to nurture a child's physical, emotional, spiritual, and mental development as they educate them academically and socially. Redefining the word *parent* to *representative*, a word that does not fall under the *Laws of Nature*, creates another abrogation to the Supreme Law of the Land and an illegal loophole for the corrupt whose goal is to remove parental rights. Though most attorneys would have you think otherwise, it is important to remember that a right can never be turned into a privilege. If the People don't pay attention to what their state legislators are drafting and how they're drafting it, then it is through their lack of involvement in politics that the pervasive erosion of the United States Constitution can take place.

Early in 2023, California State AB 957 also known as the Parental Affirmation of Transgenderism Bill was vetoed by Governor Gavin Newsom. Activists and concerned parents throughout the state jumped for joy believing that Governor Newsom had a change of heart and was finally doing the right thing in protecting parental rights; however, he was not doing the right thing. He only vetoed the bill because it was not ironclad in abolishing parental rights.

Let's look deeper into this bill to expose why he would have chosen to turn it down. This bill was designed to change the family court codes in California by compelling divorcing parents to affirm their child's transgender identity, fluidity, or expression before determining which parent would be granted custody. One of the problems with this bill is that it would criminalize one parent over the other. If one of the parents were in disagreement with the child's chosen identity and did not affirm them, the parent would be in violation of this bill and would not be granted custody. Keep in mind, family courts handle civil cases not criminal ones. A violation of this bill would be considered a criminal offense. Furthermore, government does not have the authority to compel anyone into self-incrimination by hoaxing them into waiving their 5TH Amendment right. Therefore, the primary reason this bill lacked the final stamp of approval from Governor Newsom was that if an intelligent parent chose to abstain from affirming or opposing their child's transgenderism the courts could not interpret their silence as an admission of confirmation or contention. The 5th Amendment grants everyone the right to remain silent. The judge, in this case, would be forced to maintain the previous status quo of Family Court Codes and the bill would be nullified. Every author, co-author, sponsor, and anyone who voted in favor of passing this bill failed to protect the rights of the People because this bill pressures parents into self-incrimination by way of government induced coercion.

Now, let's look at one more example. This one I believe is the most vile and heinous. It is of the LGBTQ+ community and that of their pronouns.

Up and down the state of California on my campaign trail in 2022 I kept hearing, "Who cares, let them use pronouns. It's really not such a big deal." Unfortunately, it is a big deal. Pronouns are used a multitude of times in the U.S. Constitution, Bill of Rights, and the Declaration of Independence as well as every state constitution. First, we need to look at what a pronoun is at its most basic definition. Under the Merriam Webster Dictionary, a pronoun is "a word that is used instead of a noun or noun phrase. Pronouns refer to either a noun that has already been mentioned or to a noun that does not need to be named specifically." Secondly, the use of a plural pronoun to identify a singular noun does not exist in the English language under the *Laws of Nature*, but they/them is currently being used as a reference to identify a singular person or entity. Thirdly, under the *Laws of Nature* there are only two sexes, male and female. That's not up for debate. Nature only provides for XX or XY chromosomes. Even XXY chromosomes also known as Klinefelter Syndrome and XYY trisomy only happens to males due to the presence of the XY chromosomes. XXX trisomy, therefore, only happens in females due to the presence of only XX chromosomes. Either way, XX or XY is what nature provides. Your chromosomes do not lie. You are either male or female. That is science based in fact.

At the time of this writing, there are over 80 different types of gender identity constructs. There are some in the LGBTQ+ community that would argue that the characteristics of your genitalia have nothing to do with your gender identity. This is nothing more than the splitting of hairs in order to create a new faction of humankind citizenry. The reason why this is so erroneous is because the language doesn't exist within the founding documents of our nation for such identities. When reading law, the courts will primarily adhere to originalism or the original meaning of a word or phrase at the time when it was first adopted. Originalism provides the greatest level of context. Changing a meaning of an original connotation on the basis of an emotional whim because one feels a certain way is mute to facts and disrupts linguistical canons. It sets new legislative precepts in order to maintain control of a desired narrative at any cost irrelevant if that precept is based in fantasy. This allows corrupt legislators to confound what has already been laid out before the people of this country. If the LGBTQ+ community can convince the U.S. government to legitimize their faction of a new humankind of citizenry, then legislators can have a field day undermining unalienable rights. However, this debate loses its momentum because the U.S. Constitution protects ALL rights and immunities to ALL peoples despite any chosen gender identity, fluidity, or expression.

CHAPTER 3

WE ARE AT WAR

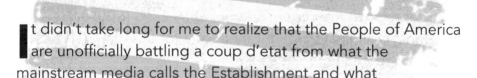

I t didn't take long for me to realize that the People of America are unofficially battling a coup d'etat from what the mainstream media calls the Establishment and what "conspiracy theorists" have labeled the Deep State.

While on the campaign trail toward the 2026 gubernatorial race in California, I would ask during my speeches if the group felt America was at war. The consensus was a deafening yes, regardless of political party. I started to explore why people thought we were in such dire conflict. The People would tell me they came to that conclusion because they felt we were in several different types of altercations. The primary battle in their perspective was the degradation of the People's authority over government. They were witnessing this happening at an alarming rate in their communities. Farmers postulated that we are in an agricultural and natural resource war. Conservative parents and teachers declared we are in an educational and child sexual indoctrination war. Investment brokers and wealth moguls asserted we are in an economic war. Activists and freedom fighters shouted that we are in a policy making political war. Church pastors and other holy leaders divulged that we are in the middle of the greatest spiritual war that is about to escalate disastrously.

Now let me ask you, do you think we are at war? If you do, how involved are you willing to get before our nation falls prey to a civil war, revolutionary war, or world war implemented by deceptive perpetrators? It is imperative that you answer this because it is that arsenal war that we are on the precipice of engaging in.

Most veterans across our nation have yet to truly involve themselves with the current state of affairs and for good reason. Veterans have already fought their wars for this nation. A couple of retired veterans said to me once,

> "If you, the People of America, screw this nation over because of your own stupidity the fault is on you, not us. We did our part. Now you do yours."

Another said,

> "Most vets have no problem embracing the suck and doing what is necessary if it means to set things right even at the cost of our own lives. We have nothing more to prove because we've already honorably proven it."

Another vet carried on and said,

> "You'd better set the bullsh-t right or picking up arms will be the only last option left even if government sh-t sandwiches the 2nd Amendment."

And still another raspy voiced vet told me,

"Wait till America's weakness and this stupid wokeness takes full effect. You will have no choice but to make a hole for U.S. veterans who will be forced to fight in your stead least you screw that up too. If that happens, don't complain when the meat-eaters bring death to your door front. There will be zero rack out until it's over. Trust me!"

The difficulty with what we're enduring as a nation is that it's hard to understand the enemies plan. If we knew the plan, maybe we could have better strategies against the multiple fronts we are being attacked from. If we knew exactly who we were up against, then maybe we could pin point our counterattacks against those individuals, departments, and agencies. We are at a disadvantage.

We need to seek a different kind of wisdom, greater than our own, to identify the best approach to confronting this fight. The corruption we are enduring will not simply be solved by attempting to appeal to a better side of our representatives. The current political representatives in our government do not have a better side. If they did, we wouldn't be in this mess. I believe in order for us to maximize the damage against our domestic enemies, we need to first realize there is an undermining of our U.S. Constitution and state constitution(s). We also need to remember how sovereignty is profoundly tied to the Bible and its prophecies. The real enemy is revealed in the Bible in 2 Corinthians Chp.4 v.4 (NLT) which states,

> "**Satan**, who is the **god of this world**, has blinded the minds of those who don't believe." (Emphasis mine).

Furthermore, the Bible is very distinct that Satan charges those who are willing to do his bidding. Ephesians Chp.2 v.2 (NASB) reveals that,

> "...according to the **prince of the power of the air,** of the spirit that is now working in the **sons of disobedience.**" (Emphasis mine).

The Bible imparts that we are dealing with Satan also known as the *god of this world* who is the *prince of the power of the air* and his workings within the *sons of disobedience.* They are the enemy that hide in plain sight who further deceive the People who don't believe.

Now that I have given you a rough idea as to who the enemies are, we can look deeper into what the ultimate purpose is behind their plan in order to best prepare a defense against it.

CHAPTER 4

THE PLAN

The plan is extremely simple, permanently remove unalienable rights endowed by the Creator so that no one can be redeemed. Without those endowments, enslavement will easily ensnare a people which is almost always followed by certain death.

Before I break down the plan, we need to take a quick look at one of the most famous and prophetic Bible verses few truly grasp and is often heavily taken out of context. Revelation Chp.14 v.9-10 (AKJV) says,

> "…If any man worship **the beast** and **his image,** and receive **his mark in his forehead,** or **in his hand,** the same shall drink of the wine of the wrath of God, which is poured out without mixture into the cup of his indignation; and he shall be tormented with fire and brimstone in the presence of the holy angels, and in the presence of the Lamb." (Emphasis mine).

Let's focus on the key word *in*. The verse states *in* their forehead or *in* their hand. The Authorized King James Version is one of the few translations that appropriately interprets the mark being administered internally. It is evident that the mark is something that must be placed inside the human body and is extremely specific as to which body parts this mark must be placed into. The only way to insert this mark would be by a medically invasive procedure of some kind. I surmise that we are looking at a type of injection that could be used to administer this mark.

The argument is often made that this mark is metaphorical or spiritual and not physical. This line of reasoning is futile because a physical action must take place to have a mark made in the forehead or hand. There are several individuals who stand against this possibility of a physical mark, but let the Bible interpret the Bible and let the wisdom of the Holy Spirit guide your understanding. It says in Revelation Chp.16 v.2 (NKJV),

> "So the first (Angel) went and poured out his bowl upon the earth, and **a foul** and **loathsome sore came upon the men who had the mark of the beast** and those who worshiped his image." (Emphasis mine).

There is no arguing against the *mark of the beast* being a physical mark that will be inserted under the skin. A metaphorical or spiritual mark would not cause a *foul* and *loathsome sore* upon those who accept the mark. *Foul* and *loathsome sores* are a negative physical reaction to what the human body is rejecting.

God will reveal His truth to you as stated in Mathew Chp.13 v.35 (KJV),

> "That it might be fulfilled which was spoken by the prophet, saying, **I will open** my mouth **in parables**; I will utter things which have been kept

secret from the foundation of the world."
(Emphasis mine).

Because the Bible defines and interprets its own meaning, the few areas we know to be allegorical are only found when Jesus is speaking in parables. Otherwise, the Bible is spoken in literalism. With this understanding, we can determine that the *mark of the beast* is indeed a literal and physical mark. This mark does not just pop-up out of nowhere. In order for this mark to be introduced properly, it must be done over a period of time. Much like the boiling frog syndrome, I believe the temperature has been turned up to the final degree upon the people of our world. In my humble opinion, one of the last few remaining steps that the mark requires to function properly has already been deceptively implemented. Sadly, millions across the world have accepted it into their bodies. I will admit this plan of a three-prong attack has been simultaneously and quite seamlessly executed.

We should all remind ourselves of who it is that we are exactly dealing with when living through these uproarious trials. Satan is the *god of this world* who is an extremely *wise* cherub. Ezekiel Chp.28 v.12-17 (NKJV) describes Satan as,

> "...the seal of perfection, full of **wisdom** and perfect in beauty. You were in Eden, the garden of God; every precious stone was your covering...You were the **anointed cherub** who covers; I established you; you were on the holy mountain of God... You were perfect in your ways from the day you were created, till iniquity was found in you...Your heart was lifted up because of your beauty; you corrupted **your wisdom** for the

sake of your splendor; I cast you to the ground."
(Emphasis mine).

Satan is directing the *sons of disobedience* to carry out these attacks on the people and every innocence across all nations. What exactly is this three-prong attack he has begun to carry out?

The first prong of the attack is to lower the intelligence of the image in order to take hold of the innocence. People ask, including many self-proclaimed Christians, who is the image? The answer is that we are the image. Humans are made in the likeness of the Creator, God the Father. We are made in His image as Genesis Chp.1 v.26 (KJV) states,

> "And God said, let us make man in **our image**, after our **likeness**." (Emphasis mine).

They also ask, who is the innocence? Our posterity is the innocence. It is our future generations. In short, the innocence are children. If you can shatter the innocence of a child, you can eradicate the future of an entire nation. I find the last sentence of Hosea Chp.4 v.6 (KJV) extremely disturbing and one that cannot be overlooked. It says,

> "My people are destroyed for **lack of knowledge**: because thou hast rejected knowledge, I will also reject thee, that thou shalt be no priest to me: seeing thou hast **forgotten the law of thy God**, I will also **forget thy children**." (Emphasis mine).

All anyone has to do is look around and observe how the youngest of our generations are heavily bombarded with wokeism, progressive liberal ideologies that gears and brainwash young minds to promote and accept Socialism, Marxism, and Communism which are the very antithesis of America's Constitution. There is a grand effort to push the normalization of pedophilia, gender dysphoria, safe spaces, and the identification of being called by a pronoun of your choice. The majority of our younger generations have come to hate their own country as well. Of course, there is much more indoctrination going on. Worst of all, these indoctrinators are venomous about a Creator and need the idea of God out of their lives. Worse yet, they are all deceptively and forcibly trying to remove God out of everyone's lives.

The sexual indoctrination of our children can be seen as teachers have taken kids on school field trips to drag queen strip clubs without parental consent. Parents who do consent, in my view, have engaged in child abuse. Too many parents have been misled down this horrific path that exposure to drag queen performances are perfectly innocent and now cheer on and applaud child drag queen performers. They allow money to be tossed at those child queen entertainers like an exotic dancer. Back in San Diego during my early twenties, I had personally witnessed parents permitting the performance of sexual lascivious acts in front of the eyes of their own children during a pride parade or some other LGBTQ+ public event I was invited to.

What you do behind closed doors with another consenting adult is not my business and is your right to privacy. I am not your judge. However, what you do in public and in front of the eyes of the innocent is my business. It is every sane adult's business to protect all children from lewd exposures. I personally will forever stand against the deviance. Let a child be

LUCIFER ZENITH / DANIEL R. MERCURI

a child. Leave the children alone.

Furthermore, California, in comparison with all other states in America has experienced the most school shootings with at least one injured victim or death since 2012. Since 2012 to the time of writing this book, there have been 664 school shooting incidents nationwide that resulted in at least one victim killed or physically wounded. According to data from the K-12 School Shooting Database, 53 incidents took place in **California**, 52 in Texas, 45 in Illinois, and 36 in Florida. These shootings were not just by adults or crazed individuals who had no relation to members of the school, but were students assaulting their own classmates and teachers. Children are the most susceptible when a nation removes God and a void is then created diminishing the value of life.

The attack on our young is also heavily present inside our state governments. For example, I've read the state senate floor notes on California's SB 145 and it is extremely misleading. This bill was spearheaded by California State Senator Scott Wiener. The reason I say the bill was misleading is simple. You have to look at the language the political officials are using to confuse their constituents. Senator Scott Wiener in his own words tweeted,

> "I'm introducing a bill (#SB 145) to end discrimination against #LGBT young ppl regarding sex offender registration. Currently, LGBT young ppl who have consensual sex w/ a person age 15-17 must register, whereas similarly situated straight young ppl don't have to."

Senator Wiener used the phrase *young people (ppl)*. The word *young people (ppl)* is subjective! This was Wiener's poor attempt to convince constituents that he's talking about an 18 or 19-year-old *young* person. He was not. He also combines that phrase with "consensual sex w/ a person age 15-17." Notice he doesn't say the word minor, child, or children. This is because there is no such thing as a consenting minor with an adult because they are minors. Last time I checked, teenagers 15-17 are still minors. They are children who are not yet legal adults. This phrasing is designed to make you think the bill is about two consenting minors which is hidden under the guise of discrimination against the LGBTQ+ community's *young people*. The real underlining argument is between adult to minor homosexual anal and oral intercourse versus heterosexual vaginal adult to minor intercourse because they are not judged the same way within the court system. Weiner's bill does not equalize criminal behavior on both for wrongful engagement with a minor. Instead, the bill removes the judicial punishment of sex offender registration on adult to minor homosexual intercourse and permits a 10-year age gap, not to go beyond 14 years of age, between adult and minor sexual criminality as long as the minor is consensual which is left to a judge's discretion. The penalty is now less of a crime. This is a deliberate act against minors. This is sick! What's next? A 15-year age gap? How about a 20-year age gap? I'm sure that is on the horizon.

There are more California bills of similar nature coming out at record speed. Between 2019 and 2020, California drafted over 4,500 bills of which over 800 of those bills were signed into law. Between 2021 and 2022 over 5,700 bills were drafted. This is how we know and can come to understand that God is truly forgetting a generation of children because we have forgotten His law that He has given unto us which has been written in the hearts of men.

To briefly digress, it astounds me that America only gives one day of remembrance to fallen military service members and one day for veterans who have all sacrificed, bled, or died for this nation. Yet, it celebrates and recognizes a salacious lifestyle for an entire month to commemorate the sexual attraction towards the same sex and gender euphoric expressions all in the name of pride. A pride flag has never had to bleed for any of America's freedoms. It benefits from the lives of those who honorably served. Proverbs Chp.16 v.18 (KJV) reminds us that

> "**Pride** goeth **before destruction**, and a haughty spirit **before a fall**." (Emphasis mine).

The second prong attack is to confound the laws by changing the meaning of WHAT IS in order to confuse the image, to confuse you. Earlier I've said that the corrupt in government like to change the language to change perception. Daniel Chp.7 v.25 (ASV) tells us,

> "…he shall speak words against the Most High, and shall wear out the saints of the Most High; and **he shall think to change** the times and the law; and they shall be given into his hand until a time and times and half a time." (Emphasis mine).

This is prophetic proof that in order for the laws to be changed to bring about an inversion to God's Law, it must be done by giving new meaning to everyday words. Let me give you a few examples. In America the con-artists in office no longer want the People to say **prison** or **jail**, it must be addressed as a **correctional facility**. They despise the term **gun control**. Instead, they **prefer gun violence prevention**. Of course, anything having to do with any form of gun control must never be referred to as an **infringement upon our 2nd Amendment**. Instead, the corrupt shift the language to the phrasing of **banning assault weapons**. Please name me one weapon that wasn't designed to assault. They're all designed to assault. That is why it's called a weapon. The language becomes even more confounded when we no longer refer to a type of pistol as a **gun**, but rather a **firearm**. Another example occurred during the Wuhan virus/Covid-19 **lock downs** when government announced to their constituents a **Stay at Home Safe Order**. Government considers the term **illegal alien** to be racist. We must now recognize illegals as **undocumented non-U.S. citizens** or **newcomers**. Daily our country continues to go down a destructive rabbit hole and asks the People to stop calling others who have an addiction **drug abuser**. Instead, we must adhere to their sensitive nature and say they have a **substance use disorder**. Don't you dare get caught saying **gay community**. It's now **LGBTQQIP2SSIA+** community. Sadly, many laws are coming out where you could be fined or imprisoned if you call someone Sir, Ma'am, or maybe even miss-genderized them by saying he or she incorrectly according to their chosen gender identifier. We must affirm **A-gender, Pan-gender, Gender Neutral, Cis-Gender, Demi-Gender, Gender Fluid, Inter-gender, Poly-gender, Non-Binary**, and even a **Maverique**. Don't confuse the term Maverique to be referring to Tom Cruise and Top Gun, but rather it is a gender that is outside the gender spectrum. Worst yet, the perverts in office and Big Tech are pushing to remove the word **pedophile** and substituting it with the word phrasing of **MAP's** (Minor Attracted Persons). This is how the *god of this world* thinks to change His laws by changing the language.

The third prong attack is to exploit the *Contract Clause* of the United States Constitution to pervert God's image and re-present Lucifer's image.

I remember as a child laughing at the absurdity of the Devil making contracts when watching Saturday morning cartoons. The Devil would come onto the screen and ask the other character to sign the Devil's contract if the character wanted a wish to come true and that it must be signed with the character's blood.

My favorite example of a Devil's contract stems from the movie Crossroads starring Ralph Macchio as Eugene, a student of classical music, and Joe Seneca as Willie Brown, a retired blues player. Eugene, a wannabe blues-guitar virtuoso finds an old blues player whom he hopes can teach him a long-lost song by legendary musician Robert Johnson. Willie Brown at a young age goes to a distant crossroad to sell his soul under contract to a person named Scratch, who we later realize is the Devil, in exchange for fame and musical talent. Eugene makes an agreement with Scratch to compete against another guitarist as to who has the better talent and give up Eugene's soul if he loses. But if he wins, Eugene keeps his soul and saves Willie's from eternal damnation.

Little did I know that the cartoons and this particular movie were revealing a truth. Lucifer is operating through the *sons of disobedience*, who do the will of their father to skillfully use contracts in order to keep God's people ignorant from the Way, the Truth, and the Life. John Chp.8 v.44 (ESV) says of these *sons of disobedience*,

> "You are of your father **the devil**, and **your will** is to do your father's desires. He was a murderer from the beginning, and **does not stand** in the truth, because there is **no truth** in him." (Emphasis mine).

It has become my firm belief that the exploitation of the *Contract Clause* is at the epicenter of everything gone wrong. It is saturating all three branches of our government and continues to spread like a cancer destroying our nation.

CHAPTER 5

RULES OF ENGAGEMENT

I believe there is another deceitful plot to further the separation of our country. It is through the widening gap between the affluent versus the destitute. Those that live a less prosperous life start to loathe those who are able to whether life's storms. I come from a common mind-set that if I am blessed then it is my duty to go out and be a blessing to others. When blessings are stolen by a vicious polity, it forces the people to reserve their remaining blessings for themselves and their families. When government policies oppress the People, they are no longer willing to get involved, help their communities, donate time, resources, or money which fuels further division.

It has been extremely difficult to listen to the howling grievances of the People of my state. The defunct Californian authorities ignore the cries of their constituents. I've lost count how many individuals have come to me and begged me for an explanation as to why I think their elected officials would blatantly and openly defy their communities. I admit, I didn't understand it either during the early stages of my journey toward political office. It was as if all authoritative agencies were playing by a different set of rules. The People of my state, myself included, needed to understand the purpose behind their defiance. My search for an answer led me down several unexpected rabbit holes. When I discovered the truth of the matter, I was surprised to know that our representatives are not playing by a different set of rules. We just don't know, nor have we ever been taught, the rules of engagement. The People of the United States misunderstand chess for checkers. You cannot play by the rules of a game that are not on the board.

I discovered that there was a historic biblical event that took place that established those rules, exposed who established it, and what the final prime directive is. This prime directive is something we must keep at the ready when we find ourselves caught in the middle of an onslaught by these unethical operatives. I do not believe in coincidences. In fact, the root word of coincidence is to coincide. I believe that God was using this event to reveal those truths for those seeking answers. The event that sets up the initial rules of engagement is laid out before us in the book of Job. Job Chp.1 v.6-12 (NASB1995) states,

> "Now there was a day when the sons of God came to present themselves before the LORD, and Satan also came among them. The LORD said to Satan, '**From where do you come?**' Then Satan answered the LORD and said, '**From roaming about on the earth and walking around on it.**' The LORD said to Satan, 'Have you considered My servant Job? For there is no one like him on the Earth, a blameless and upright man, fearing God and turning away from evil.' Then Satan answered the LORD, 'Does Job fear God for nothing? Have You not made a hedge about him and his house and all that he has, on every side? You have blessed the work of his hands, and his possessions have increased in the land. **But put forth Your**

hand now and touch all that he has; he will surely curse You to Your face.' Then the LORD said to Satan, **'Behold, all that he has is in your power, only do not put forth your hand on him.'** So, Satan departed from the presence of the LORD." (Emphasis mine).

This is one of the most fascinating verses of the Bible and not for the reasons many have thought. The Lord asks Satan, "From where do you come?" Several people would debate that God is proving He is not omniscient in posing that question; however, that is not the case. What the Lord proves by His question to Lucifer is that Satan cannot lie to the Father. It would be fruitless. Not only does God force Satan to prove his whereabouts to the other heavenly hosts present, but He constrains Lucifer to tell Him the truth as Lucifer answers, "From roaming about on the earth and walking around on it." In this rare moment, Satan speaks the truth. If he had lied to the Lord, he would have been lying to himself.

As God and Lucifer continue their discussion about Job, Satan points out that if God "put forth (His) hand" meaning took all of Job's blessings away from him, Job would curse God to His face. Many pastors and theologians would agree that Satan's words are a challenge to God. A small bet essentially is waged to decide whether or not Job would curse God if He decided to remove all of Job's blessings. It is brilliant how our heavenly Father turns the table and allows Lucifer to do the bidding himself as He says, "Behold, all that he has is in your power, only do not put forth your hand on him." Lucifer, being so smug with himself, believed he could succeed with Job. This is where we see the first few initial rules laid out before us. Satan was permitted by God that he could destroy the blessings of

45

Job, but Satan was not permitted to touch or harm Job directly. Job was physically off limits to Satan. This proves that Lucifer only has the power God permits him to wield. When reading all of Job, Lucifer abided by the rules. Nowhere in the book of Job does Satan deviate from the rules. Why? It is because he can't deceive God and it confirms that there are rules Satan is required to follow even to this very day. If Satan has to follow a set of rules, so must his followers who are the *sons of disobedience*.

We know that Lucifer is the Great Deceiver and the world's greatest liar, but God reveals that Lucifer has to tell the truth when speaking to Him. The book of Job also reveals that heavenly hosts can challenge one another. In the case of Job, the wager was to curse or not to curse. These verses showcase that when any challenge is made against God's image, His masterpiece, rules are laid out that the enemy is required to follow and cannot deviate from. Nowhere in the Bible does Lucifer deviate from a single rule God sets before him. Those rules are God's Law and it is He who set up the true rules of ALL laws written in the hearts of men.

In the United States per American judicial doctrine, the courts will utilize *stare decisis* which is Latin for *to stand by things decided. Stare decisis* means that if it was made good law once and a similar situation arises, it will be made good law again. This occurs with the case of Job. It has always been Lucifer's primary goal to have all of God's children shake their fists to the heavens and curse God to His face choosing damnation over His grace and salvation which he attempted to do with Job. Satan needs to obscure what the final prime directive is. This makes it imperative that we know and understand it in order for us to properly fight against the evils we face today.

In the most simplistic and genius of strategies, God lays out for Satan a rule God Himself abides by as we read in Amos Chp.3 v.7 (NIV) that

> "Surely the Sovereign **Lord does nothing without revealing His plan** to **His servants** the prophets." (Emphasis mine).

This verse tells us that the Lord does nothing without "revealing His plans to His servants." This means Lucifer, O' Son of the Morning, must also reveal his plans before he does it. One caveat I must point out is that the Lord God never says in the Bible HOW Satan must reveal his plan. He just requires that it must be revealed. This is where Satan and the *sons of disobedience* work their deception. These deceivers who have corrupted governments across the world, operate within the rule of law by WHEREVER IT'S NOT SAID. Wherever IT IS said, is where they change the language to change perception in order to pass repugnant legislation so they can legitimize their betrayal.

Now many of you may be asking, when and where did or does Satan reveal his plans? Confusion is the Devil's playground. It may be hard to believe, but these deceitful clandestine agents reveal their plans through mainstream news outlets, magazines, online articles, movies, television shows and advertisements, social media, and live-streams. Their mouthpieces are musicians, actors, show hosts, models, business moguls, and star politicians. The reason why most people, including Christians, don't see their plans hiding in plain sight is because we're all bombarded with purposeful distraction. Their plans, like an artist, are hidden in their performance rituals staged by way of dances, symbols, secret handshakes, contracts, coded language, policies, literature, numbers, and advertising imagery. We see and hear their plans every day. We are just too busy being…entertained.

There are too many movies, songs, business logos, and symbols hiding in plain sight. I will only reveal a handful to make my point. Many have heard of the Luciferian All-Seeing Eye also known as the Eye of Providence or the Eye of Horus. It is a single human eye enclosed by a triangle. Countless times we've seen celebrities form this triangle with their hands over one of their eyes or they have covered up one eye using their hand, hair, a photographer's artistry on a music label or front cover of a magazine, or on movie posters in shadow. It is their way of publicly paying homage to their *god of this world*, Lucifer. For years, the Freemasons have denied that the symbol of the All-Seeing Eye hovering over the pyramid on the $1 bill is in any way, shape, or form Masonic. As of late, official Masonry is now bragging to their members that this is precisely the case! After 1797, the very mysterious order of the Freemasons started using the Eye of Providence as a public symbol of their strength, influence, and power. The veil is lifting. But who do these Luciferians, Rosicrucian, Illuminati, Freemasons, Skull and Bones, and other clandestine secret societies that are the *sons of disobedience* control? Look no further than your television. The word television is hiding their power in plain sight because they are Telling-You-A-Vision. It is their vision of a plan they intend on enacting before they do it. This is another reason why they call it a television program because they are programming the mind. They are desensitizing the watcher so it appears that these secret Elites' destructive actions are nothing more than coincidental occurrences.

How can we be sure the *sons of disobedience* control the airways? Remember, Lucifer is known as the *prince of the power of the air*. We are not just talking about a heavenly host taking flight. If we look at a few major television broadcast logos, we can see who they belong too. The Columbia Broadcast System's (CBS) logo is the All-Seeing Eye that is the representation of the Eye of Horus or Providence. The American Broadcasting Company's (ABC) logo is written in the center of a black circle eye. The black eye represents the unknown and the hidden secrets that lie beyond our understanding that are heavily used in occultism. The National Broadcasting Company's (NBC) logo is a rainbowed peacock. What are on a peacock's feathers? Eyes! The cable company Time Warner Spectrum's logo was also the All-Seeing Eye shaped as the Egyptian Eye of Ra. The company denied that claim and said it was an eye overlapping an ear. Years later, they changed their logo to a triangle of all things.

When viewed from above, the Creative Arts Agency (CAA) building in Los Angeles which is one of the largest Hollywood talent and sport agencies in the world, incorporates the one eye and Freemasonry symbols into its architecture. The buildings themselves are pyramidal in design. There is one eye inside a pyramid in the lower courtyard and another one eye displayed on the grounds in front of the entrance. The architectural design also appears to have a snake bordering it when viewed from a google digital sky view of the area. A quick side note, the CAA building is on the cross streets of Avenue of the Stars and Olympic Boulevard. They are displaying who their allegiance is to. Of course, they will not boldly admit to the public that Lucifer is their god. This is why you must have eyes to see and ears to hear.

What if I told you that the *sons of disobedience* divulged one of their horrid visions in a Hollywood movie back in 2011? The summary of this movie is about the spread of a highly contagious virus that would be transmitted by respiratory droplet and fomites. Frantic attempts would be made by medical researchers and public health officials to identify and contain the disease that will cause the loss of social order as the virus turns into a worldwide pandemic and the introduction of a vaccine will be the surviving key to halting its spread. This sounds eerily similar to the Wuhan/Covid-19 pandemic. The movie plot was from the blockbuster thriller called, Contagion. Again, there is no such thing as a coincidence. They have to tell you their plans before they do it because it is His law. Remember, wherever it's not said is HOW they reveal their plans before they execute it.

CHAPTER 6

LAWS, STATUTES, & VESTED POWERS

The Wuhan/Covid-19 virus shut down the world's economy. Every nation experienced an insurmountable number of mandates, regulations, health code violation fines, and fees that cunningly coerced the People out of their right to life, liberty, and the pursuit of happiness. In fact, the government took everyone's rights and sabotaged the People's authority the heaviest during that time. Remember, when the People don't know their rights, they have no rights. When the People don't know the Law, there is no Law. In fact, every government official throughout the nation that supported Stay at Home Safe ORDERS violated their oath. Each one of them should no longer be holding their seated positions and should be criminally charged in an Article III tribunal.

Throughout my campaigns, it became clear to me that the People are unfortunately unaware of the differences between what is law and what is statute. As an everyday individual, it is fundamentally important to understand the basics between the two. The United States Constitution defines the limitation of powers. It does not grant our representatives more charge, more authority, or more power to further their own agendas. Article I. Sec. 8 lists out 18 clauses. 17 of those clauses enumerate relatively specific powers granted to Congress.

These jurisdictions cannot be expanded on by Congress nor any other state legislature. If and when this occurs, it is an act of usurpation. Any and all usurpations are null and void.

Keep in mind that the status of People and the Will of the People are above government at all times. When we look at mandates, regulations, codes, polices, orders, ordinances, and statutes their primary function is to control the behavior of all government officials, federal and state agencies, and commercial activities. Nowhere did the Framers of our great nation allow for the behavior of people to be controlled by government. It does not exist in the composition of our government. However, the People find themselves inundated with egregious legislation that would force mandates, regulations, codes, policies, orders, ordinances, and statutes to operate in such a way that they would control the behavior of the People. If these legislations take place, then those breaches would abrogate the *Laws of Nature and of Nature's God*. Such unlawful enforcements make it impossible to have a nation under God because government would be superseding and repudiating His law.

When referring to law, we are talking about God's Law or what we would also call Common Law. Common Law is the true law of the land. Our Framers understood that His law was written in the hearts of men. Nature's God provided common decree within all people. We all know that murder is wrong and it is, therefore, common to all people. Stealing is wrong and is, therefore, common to all people. Lying is wrong and is, therefore, common to all people. Those behaviors do not need to be taught that they are wrong because they are innately wrong to all people.

Statutes are legislative laws your representatives draft that SHALL harmonize with the Supreme Law of the Land. The courts have expressed that the legislature must engage in clarity for proper interpretive effect. The drafting of any statute starts and ends with the language and structure of the statute. Ambiguity is unwelcomed by all courts because the prescribed language must be harmonious with linguistical canons that do not confound words being used in their common inferences at the time a phrase or word became prevalent. This is why I stated earlier that they, the corrupt in government, like to change the language to change perception to pass repugnant legislation. Ignorance is their de-facto weaponry. Looking at the root word of ignorance means to simply ignore. These swine in office are keenly aware that the majority of people ignore their duty to be wisely informed about any potential illicit activities taking place within the walls of lewd governance. Office holders are in-tune to the fact that their constituents truly don't understand the basic foundation of any law, let alone His law. Ingeniously, they deceptively substitute the true law of the land for treacherous statutes which are nothing more than political liberty not natural liberty.

The Supremacy Clause, Article VI. Paragraph 2 of the U.S. Constitution, establishes that the federal constitution takes precedence over statutes and state constitutions. Simply put, all legislation and court rulings must harmonize with the Supreme Law of the Land which is Common Law. Similarly, the state constitution represents the highest legal authority of the state. The state may then enact state statutes which apply to everyone within the state. State statutes cannot violate the state constitution, the federal constitution, or federal law. No code can be enacted or enforced if it is not properly uniform to the state constitution. If a statute is out of sync with any of the aforementioned, there must be a rectification. This disparity between statutes, constitutions, and federal law happens far too often and only serves to protect government officials and not the People.

If statutes are also referred to as codes that are not regulatory or administrative, then why are so many misnomers used when they fall under the umbrella of principled actions of governance? This is a tactical action utilized by the corrupted legislators because making legislative language more straightforward would help people understand their rights and obligations better. The People would be less susceptible to unnecessary punishment and could prevent lawmakers from infringing upon the People's entitlements. Government entities choose to inflate the legal jargon in an ultimate attempt to subvert His authority. All other intentions are peripheral.

American Jurisprudence (Am.Jur.) is a multi-volume national legal encyclopedia. The contents of Am.Jur. include state and federal legal topics which are alphabetically arranged in more than 400 subjects and chapters. Book 16 Am.Jur. 2d., Sec. 98 states,

> "...an **emergency cannot**, and no emergency justifies the violation of any of the provisions of the United States Constitution or State's Constitution(s)." (Emphasis mine).

This means no emergency has just cause to suppress the U.S. Constitution or State Constitution. You may recall that the Wuhan/Covid-19 Virus was issued as a national EMERGENCY and all states declared their own State of Emergency! When the government ORDERED its people to stay at home, they violated their oath because officials are not granted permission to control behavior. Preventing sovereigns from physical mobility is a controlled behavior. Our representative's job was to work around the pandemic, not to try and subjugate the authority and rights of the People. It was by the threat of the Wuhan/Covid-19 pandemic that on March 4, 2020, Governor Gavin Newsom proclaimed a State of Emergency to be implemented in California. The following are a few of California Governor Gavin Newsom's 2020 Executive Orders during the pandemic:

E.O. N33-20, the Stay at Home Safe Order

E.O. N67-20, the Vote by Mail Order. *This was used to pass AB-860 Mail-in-Ballot Bill.*

E.O. N09-21, the Masks and Physical Distancing Order

These orders violate the U.S. Constitution in Article IV. Sec. 2 which states that

"the Citizens of each State **shall** be entitled to **all** Privileges and Immunities of Citizens in the several States." (Emphasis mine).

All three executive orders attempt to control mobility, behavior, entitlement (also known as rights), and immunities (also known as exemptions). These orders are void acts because they are inconsistent with valid law and cannot operate when they supersede constitutional rights.

Governor Newsom's executive orders were in violation with the

U.S. Constitution Article VI. which states,

> "This Constitution, and the Laws of the United States which shall be made in Pursuance thereof; and all Treaties made, or which shall be made, under the Authority of the United States, shall be the **Supreme Law of the Land**; and the Judges in every State shall be bound thereby, any Thing in the Constitution or Laws of any State to the **Contrary notwithstanding**." (Emphasis mine).

He breached the confines of the limitation to his power listed in Article VI. Let's look further into the terms utilized in this article to understand why this statement is true. Merriam Webster's Dictionary defines the word *notwithstanding* to mean *despite* or *in spite of*. The word *contrary* is given the definition *opposite, contradict, or both can be false, but both cannot be true*. Therefore, *contrary notwithstanding* means no law, act, order etc. can be drafted or passed that is contradictory to the Supreme Law of the Land.

Between the years of 1930 to 2022, only 146 U.S. Supreme Court cases have ever been overturned. **Roe v. Wade** is the most recent. Only one-half of one percent of ALL U.S. Supreme Court cases were overturned during those years. Among these 146 cases, zero have been overturned due to an abrogation or abridgement of the Supreme Law of the Land. The most notable U.S. Supreme Court cases uncontested to this day are:

Murdock v. Pennsylvania (1943), 319 U.S. 105:
"No State shall convert a liberty into a license and charge a fee therefore." We call that extortion.

Miranda v. Arizona (1966), 384 U.S. 436: "Where Rights secured by the Constitution are involved, there can be no rule making or legislation which would abrogate them."

Shuttleworth v. City of Birmingham Alabama (1968), 394 U.S. 147: "If the State converts a Right (Liberty) into a privilege, the citizen can ignore the license and fee and engage in the Right (Liberty) with impunity."

The most notable U.S. Supreme Court cases unchallenged today that stem prior to 1930 are:

Marbury v. Madison (1803), 5 U.S. 137: "All laws, rules, practices which are repugnant to the Constitution are null and void."

Hoke v. Henderson (1839), 38 U.S. 230: "Statutes which would deprive a citizen of the rights of person or property without a regular trial, according to the course and usage of common law, would not be the law of the land."

Yick Wo v. Hopkins (1886), 118 U.S. 356: "**Sovereignty itself** is, of course, not subject to law, for it is the author and source of law." (Emphasis Mine).

One such example that proves nefarious operatives constantly set their aim to skirt around the limitation of powers is the California's Emergency Services Act (CESA) that was activated during the pandemic. CESA deceitfully blurs the lines of vested powers. It gives the California Governor broad ambiguous consolidated authority. The malevolent in office always hide their deception under emergencies. CESA is incompatible on a federal level with the U.S. Constitution as noted in Article I. Sec. 1 which states,

> "All legislative Powers herein granted shall be **vested** in a Congress of the United States." (Emphasis mine).

Article II. Sec. 1 says,

> "The executive Power shall be **vested** in a President of the United States of America." (Emphasis mine).

Lastly, Article III. Sec. 1 tells us that

> "The judicial Power of the United States, shall be **vested** in one supreme Court." (Emphasis mine).

We can also see how CESA is in conflict with California's own state constitution which establishes parameters for vested powers in Article III. Sec. 3 that says,

> "The powers of state government are legislative, executive, and judicial. Persons charged with the exercise of one power **may not** exercise either of the others **except** as permitted by **this Constitution.** (Emphasis mine).

Article IV. Sec. 1 also states,

"The legislative power of this State is **vested** in the California Legislature." (Emphasis mine).

CESA is not, nor could it ever be, amended in the California State Constitution to grant more charge above the vested clause established in the U.S. Constitution which is the Supreme Law of the Land above any state constitution. It is, therefore, illegal. Because the people are obtuse to the laws, government sanctions their enactments. Such flagrant deeds against the Will of the People and the authority that the People wield proves deliberate sedition. This must be stopped.

CHAPTER 7

WHERE THE CORRUPT IN GOVERNMENT HIDE & OPERATE

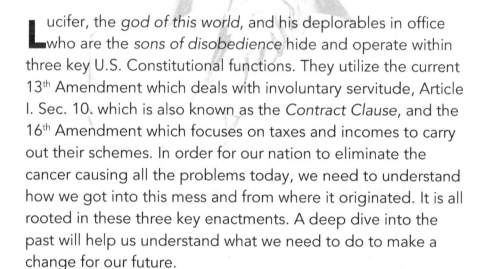

Lucifer, the *god of this world*, and his deplorables in office who are the *sons of disobedience* hide and operate within three key U.S. Constitutional functions. They utilize the current 13th Amendment which deals with involuntary servitude, Article I. Sec. 10. which is also known as the *Contract Clause*, and the 16th Amendment which focuses on taxes and incomes to carry out their schemes. In order for our nation to eliminate the cancer causing all the problems today, we need to understand how we got into this mess and from where it originated. It is all rooted in these three key enactments. A deep dive into the past will help us understand what we need to do to make a change for our future.

Let's take a closer look at the original 13th Amendment. The current 13th Amendment was in fact the original 14th Amendment. It was shuffled into the 13th position so the presently active 14th Amendment, a new erroneous jurisdiction, could quietly chip away and supplant the People's sovereignty. The original 13th Amendment was thought to have been destroyed at the burning of the U.S. Capitol during the War of 1812. It was later rediscovered in several of the states and territories archives. Oddly enough, it was also found in the British Museum Library. You might wonder why the original

United States of America's 13th Amendment was in the British Museum Library to begin with. In short, the Crown wasn't ready to wash their hands of America at the burgeoning time of the United States' inception. They kept record of it because they needed a more subtle way of regaining control, especially since America had become bankrupt at the time.

I will only cover a small portion of the original 13th Amendment so that it may provide clarity to the current issues at hand. It reads,

> "If any citizen of the United States, shall accept, receive, or retain any **title of nobility** or **honour**, or shall without the consent of Congress, accept and retain any present, pension, office, or **emolument** of any kind whatever, from any Emperor, King, Prince, or foreign Power, **such person shall cease to be a citizen of the United States, and shall be incapable of holding any office or trust or profit under them, or either of them.**" (Emphasis mine).

America's Founders held extreme aversion and distrust for the recognition of any *title of nobility or honour* of the privileged. The Revolutionary War was fought primarily to abolish any type of abuse, transgressions, or autocratic regimes that stemmed from *nobility and honours*. America's Founders knew they would interfere with America becoming a prosperous nation and a nation that would affirm the isonomy of a free people. Therefore, the Framers of America instituted penalties to anyone welcoming or adopting a *title of nobility or honour*.

The 13th Amendment addresses the use of emoluments, which are bribes or gifts that could be a form or type of services rendered in exchange for loyalty to a foreign government or other body of power. In essence, lobbying. The word lobbying is another purposeful change of language because they are in fact emoluments and, therefore, in violation of the original 13th Amendment. Lobbying, comes in the form of campaign donations and insider trading information given out on the backend to your representatives during their campaign trails prior to holding office or during their terms of service once in office. Activists also teach people how to lobby. This is an inaccurate use of the term because activists don't actually lobby. They petition their representatives for redresses of grievances and should separate themselves from falling prey to the detesting nature of what lobbyists engage in with emoluments.

Several history scholars have debated whether the original 13th Amendment was truly ratified. They all fail in their arguments to recognize that it was printed in the 1815 published collections of legislative acts across most jurisdictions as the standing 13th Amendment of the time. The original 13th Amendment was also believed throughout the nation to be part of the U.S. Constitution well into the nineteenth century. The other factor that should not be overlooked is that the original 13th Amendment would ban lawyers from citizenship due to their use of the title Esquire which is still utilized today. The Framers of our nation wanted to ensure that any practicing lawyer would be forced to abstain from peacocking intellectual elevation above the People. They would be subjecting themselves to a life of servitude and become the gatekeepers to American sovereignty if they so desired to truly serve their nation.

The current U.S. Constitution under Article I. Sec. 9, Clause 8 reads,

"No Title of Nobility shall be granted by the
United States: And no Person holding any Office
of Profit or Trust under them, shall, without the
Consent of the Congress, accept of any present,
Emolument, Office, or Title, of any kind whatever,
from any King, Prince, or foreign State."
(Emphasis Mine).

This clause mirrors the original 13th Amendment with one
important variance. The following penalty was not included
from the original 13th Amendment. It stated,

"…such person **shall cease to be a citizen** of the
United States, and **shall be incapable of holding
any office** or trust or profit under them, or either
of them." (Emphasis mine).

The consequence as stated in the original 13th Amendment
you've just read states that if any *title of nobility or honour* was
to be accepted and used, those individuals would cease to be
citizens and would be incapable of holding any political office.
Essentially, lawyers Esq. were unwelcomed to hold political
office.

One of the primary struggles against attorneys holding office is
that they are very good with creating obscurities and ambiguity
with their words to deliberately confound the language and
thwart defensive efforts against their potential devious
ambition. A second issue is that the title Esquire creates a
hierarchy within the judicial branch. This dismisses any self-
litigation without representation. The core definition of
representation is to be re-presented under a contrasting set of
jurisdictions. It places the status of the People under the

government and under the title of Esquire which grants a lawyer ubiquitous power of attorney. Lastly, we find that attorneys are under the rule of Corpus Juris Secundum (CJS) Volume 7, Sec. 5 that is titled Attorney & Client Relationship. It stipulates,

> "His **first duty is to the courts** and the public, **not to the clients,** and wherever the duties to his client **conflict** with those he owes as an officer of the court in the administration of justice, **the former must yield to the latter."** (Emphasis mine).

This is in conflict with the U.S. Constitution. The courts have been overrun by the American Bar Association (ABA) and are quite often out of alignment with the Supreme Law of the Land. The ABA has defined justice by way of upholding the law. Most would have no argument against that, but law and justice are not synonymous. In fact, it is not the law, but the jury's duty to ensure justice prevails. Statutory law, unless in agreement with the Supreme Law of the Land, quite often obscures a right in exchange for codified permission. This is why the U.S. Constitution under the 6th Amendment provides

> "…the right to a public and speedy trial, **by an impartial jury."** (Emphasis mine).

The Bill of Rights guarantees three kinds of juries. They are the Grand Jury according to the 5th Amendment, the Criminal Trial Jury according to the 6th Amendment, and the Civil Jury according to the 7th Amendment. All juries are comprised of the People and are considered to be an extension of the fourth branch of government by way of a Grand De Jure according to **United States v. Williams** (1992), 112 S.Ct. 1735, 504 U.S. 36,

118 L.Ed.2d 352 in which Justice Antonin Scalia, writing for the majority,

> "confirmed that the American **Grand Jury** is neither part of the judicial, executive nor legislative branches of government, but instead belongs to the people. **It is** in effect **a fourth branch of government** 'governed' and administered to directly by and on behalf of the American people, and its authority emanates from the Bill of Rights. Thus, citizens have the unbridled right to **empanel their own grand juries** and present 'True Bills' of indictment to a court, which is then required **to commence a criminal proceeding.**" (Emphasis mine).

Therefore, these juries have the final say in preserving our rights. The judiciary is absolutely barred from reversing whatever is decided by the People and it cannot be overturned.

It is little known that the courts and the criminal behavior of the transgressor in question are equally on trial. The CJS uses the word *conflict* to encourage practicing attorneys to willfully interfere with any impartial grand and petit jury by instituting loyalty to the courts first, not His law. His Law was designed to be in the hands of a jury to preserve the People's status above government while keeping all judges answerable to protecting the U.S. Constitution.

There is a chapter within the Federal Trial Handbook titled, Purpose of this Handbook. It reads on Page 5, Paragraph 2,

> "The judge will instruct the jury in each separate

case as to the law of that case. For example, in each criminal case, the **judge will tell the jury**, among other things, that a defendant charged with a crime is presumed to be innocent and the burden of proving his guilt beyond a reasonable doubt **is upon the Government. Jurors must follow** only the instructions of **law given to them by the** trial **judge** in each particular case." (Emphasis mine).

This is wrong. The judge has no legal powers to cherry pick which laws the jury should be primed to focus on. The jury derives its authority by unalienable endowment written in the hearts of men. It is cemented in the U.S. Constitution and harmonious with Federal and State Statutes, not the judge. This act alone would be considered jury tampering. However, if you are an uninformed juror you are incapable of ensuring judges don't cross into using unconstitutional, foul doctrine.

As of 2023, more than 22% of California's State Assembly and Senate were attorneys. This is the largest occupational category in the California State Legislature's listings of previous job history. This percentage of lawyers has steadily increased over the last few years. Before the founding of the California Office of Legislative Counsel in 1913, members had to write their own bills. Because lawyers were often advisors to many state representatives, this practice later popularized the assumption that lawmakers should be lawyers. This ideology has spread like a cancer to all legislative bodies that are now teaming with attorneys who essentially draft nearly every bill put onto the floor. These bills are never truly written by your representative. You must now ask yourself, who really is running the show? Many representatives have become puppets to the Bar or are members of the Bar that have destroyed impartiality of justice by proxy or cart blanch.

Now let's take a look at the current 13th Amendment. Sec. 1 says,

> "Neither slavery nor **involuntary servitude**, except as a punishment for crime whereof the party shall have been duly convicted, shall exist within the United States, or any place subject to their jurisdiction." (Emphasis mine).

The phrase *involuntary servitude* is the primary pressure point of their infiltration. This is where one of the greatest exploitations in all of corrupt government rests. Remember I said earlier, corrupt government operates *wherever it's not said*. Now we need to ask, what is not being said within the standing 13th Amendment? Voluntary servitude! Government does not have the authority to force the People into a life of slavery or involuntary servitude. This includes any form of bondage, debt labor, or peonage. However, nothing is said about volunteering one's self into a life of serfdom. This is why the original 13th Amendment was removed. It was withdrawn in order to usurp the Will of the American people, ruled by His Law. The miscreants needed a way to bring in lawyers to cunningly subvert the U.S. Constitution without denying those attorneys citizenry or the ability to hold office. But let's face one important fact, no sane individual would truly ever volunteer themselves into a life of enslavement or subjugation. How then is this deceptive undertaking achieved? It is attained through the exploitation of Article I. Sec. 10 of the U.S. Constitution also known as the *Contract Clause*. Article I. Sec. 10 reads,

> "**No State shall enter into any** Treaty, Alliance, or Confederation; grant Letters of Marque and Reprisal; coin Money; emit Bills of Credit; make any Thing but gold and silver Coin a Tender in Payment of Debts; pass any Bill of Attainder, ex post facto Law, or **Law impairing the Obligation of Contracts**, or grant any Title of Nobility."
> (Emphasis mine).

Most state constitutions have similar amendments that mirror much of the U.S. Constitution. California's *Contract Clause* in Article I. Sec. 9 reads,

> "A **bill of attainder**, ex post facto law, or **law impairing the obligation of contracts may not be passed**." (Emphasis mine).

Since "No State shall enter into any…Law impairing the Obligation of Contracts," the RIGHT to a contract is NOT LIMITED. That means any and all contracts can be completely egregious to state constitution(s) and to the Supreme Law of the Land. Under the *Contract Clause* in a Nisi Prius court and even at times within a Court of Record, judges will take the constitution and throw it out. Why? It doesn't apply. How is that possible? Remember, the contract according to the U.S. Constitution must be fulfilled. The word *obligation* is the key word. The *obligation* to fulfill that contract applies even if contracts are made in bad faith.

Additionally, the 13th Amendment allows for the omission of *voluntary servitude*. Therefore, it is permitted for private entities and government bodies to engage in *legal fraudulent concealment*. Contract illiteracy invariably falls on the receiving

69

individual. Government and corporations don't have to tell you the specifics within those contracts or the meaning behind their phrasing. The People have to figure out for themselves whether they are being treated as a constituent or a customer because generalities or overt expositions are concordat allies that work to purposely fraud the People into a life of serfdom. This is another reason why people never have to opt in, they always have to opt out. Silence is now considered agreement under their terms and conditions. These kinds of contracts are still unconstitutional. Silence is not, nor can it ever be, an admission of guilt or a confirmation of agreement. Even still, this is how contracts are sinisterly designed. Corporations and the Elites will lobby your representatives to set up bills that would favor a multitude of syndicates rather than the People. This in turn forces compliancy to commerce and compels you to become a witness against yourself. It is a dupery into getting someone to wave their 5th Amendment right. The U.S. Constitution does not allow for that. Those bills and acts impinge upon a free market and desire to control the behavior of the People. The legislature only has authority to regulate commerce and nothing more. They can't force the People to engage in commerce. Through the *Contract Clause* and the permissibility to charter *legal fraudulent concealment*, representatives can now change the language through the contract transaction on behalf of their constituents without consent. They can purposely omit information as a result of the 13th Amendment and attempt to coerce behavioral commerce with impunity.

Remember, *legal fraudulent concealment* only works if the People remain ignorant. Unfortunately, the courts are fully aware of the People's complicity. In the case of **United States v. Minker** (1956), 350 U.S. 179, it was ruled that

> "Because of what appears to be a lawful command on the **surface**, many citizens, because of their **respect** for what **only appears to be law**, are **cunningly coerced** into **waiving their Rights** due to **ignorance**." (Emphasis mine).

How does one waive their rights? No one with proper sanity would ever do that. Rights are waived by your pledge on the endorsing line of a contract. A chief reason why the People's grievances are falling on deaf ears is because of their ignorance of Article I. Sec.10. The courts have told you that they know the People pay very little, if any, attention to the government's obligatory indentured trickery of surrendering one's own individual rights.

It's no longer enough to pay attention to what is being said or written down, but rather you must pay attention to what is NOT being said and what is NOT written down. Let's take a look at another example that I believe will solidify my point about *wherever it's not said*. When people are taken into custody by law enforcement, they are usually read their Miranda Rights. We've seen people being mirandized many times in movies, television shows, and in real life situations conducted by the arresting officer. The Miranda script reads,

> "You have the right to remain silent. Anything you say **can** and **will be used against you** in a court of law. You have the right to an attorney. If you cannot afford an attorney, one will be provided for you. Do you understand the rights I have just read to you? With these rights in mind, do you wish to speak to me?" (Emphasis mine).

Pay close attention to the word phrasing, "can and will be used against you." Notice how your words will never be used for you, or in support of you, to guide you, or to help maintain your innocence? No. It's always against you. This is because of the two most important and crucial words that are invoked CAN and WILL. This is the telltale sign that all crime is commercial. Courts of Commerce are not Courts of Record.

An extending example would be when a driver at 3:00AM in the morning is out on the road and the roads are barren. The driver decides to make an illegal U-turn and a highway patrol unit witnesses the act. If the patrol unit decides to pull the driver over and site them a traffic ticket, who is the injured party? No one. There was no disruption to the flow of traffic nor an incident that would cause delay or harm to a bystander. A court maxim is that for every crime, there must be an injured party and for every injured party there must be a remedy which is required to be decided within a Court of Record by a jury of our peers. Government is not permitted to be the injured party. If the patrol officer decides to move forward in order to dispense a ticket to the driver, we would then generally call that extortion. If you sign the ticket, you are agreeing per the contract to lowering your status under the government's jurisdiction. This is why all crime has become commercial. Once a driver signs that ticket which is a government contract to appear in traffic court, the driver has now subjected themselves into waiving their rights. They have been cunningly coerced into paying the ticket fine and court fees, attending traffic school, and acquiring increased car insurance for becoming a high-risk driver. Those payouts are various forms of commercial activity. You now have a foundational understanding as to why all crime is commercial in regard to our judicial branch and why government agencies have an obligation to engage in *legal fraudulent concealment.* It is for profit!

This now leads into the third enactment that corrupt government hides and operates behind. It requires us to scrutinize the very controversial 16th Amendment. I only say controversial because several constitutionalists, historians, and researchers argue whether or not it was ratified. I will not be getting into that discussion since it is the acquired standing amendment and whether I agree or disagree with its legitimacy is a mute factor to the power it wields today. The 16th Amendment allows the U.S. government to lay and collect taxes on incomes. Pay close attention to what is written. Remember, words matter. The 16th Amendment reads,

> "The Congress shall have power to **lay** and **collect taxes** on **incomes**, from **whatever source derived**, without apportionment among the several states, and without regard to any census or enumeration." (Emphasis mine).

This amendment is truly about the contractual tax debt enslavement of income that is falsely masquerading as labor and capital. Labor and capital were distinctly separated from the term income by all three government branches from the late 1800s to the early 1900s.

We've already established that the courts utilize *stare decisis* which is Latin for *to stand by things decided.* Therefore, if an argument from a similar past case or from analogy is still standing, it is good in law and can be applied to the current case.

The Supreme Court ruled in **Butchers Union v. Crescent City**

Co. (1884), 111 U.S. 746 that

> "The property which every man has in his own
> **labor**, as it is the **original foundation** of all other
> property, so it is the most sacred and **inviolable.**"
> (Emphasis mine).

The courts are very clear in obstructing outside forces having authority over a person's labor. It was determined that it cannot be violated because labor makes capital.

During the State of the Union Address given by President Abraham Lincoln in 1861, he said,

> "**Labor** is prior to, and **independent of, capital.**
> Capital is only the fruit of labor, and could never
> have existed if **labor** had not **first existed**. Labor is
> the superior of capital, and deserves much the
> higher consideration." (Emphasis mine).

President Lincoln was simply saying that labor is self-standing and not to be confused with what was gained by that labor. The court ruling in **Knowlton v. Moore** (1900), 178 U.S. 41 says,

> "The qualification of uniformity is imposed **not**
> upon all taxes, which the Constitution authorizes,
> but only on **duties, imposts** and **excises.**"

In addition, the United States Constitution in Article I. Sec. 8 reads,

> "The Congress shall have power to lay and **collect**
> **taxes, duties, imposts** and **excises**, to pay the

debts and provide for the common defense and general welfare of the United States; but all **duties, imposts** and **excises** shall be uniform throughout the United States." (Emphasis mine).

What is now evident, is that government can only collect taxes on duties, imposts, and excises not on labor, capital, or even principal.

When the 16th Amendment was active, Congress in 1913 further explained capital as,

> "The **earnings** of any person from **any occupation** or **profession** would, if not spent in like manner, becomes **principal**. If by professional effort any person should earn a given sum annually and he spends half of it, he saves the other half. The half of so saved in turn becomes **principal. That principal is property.**" (Emphasis mine).

If any employer hires an employee, government has no dominion over the agreed upon payment between the two. The employee's earnings are considered *inviolable*. The savings of what is left of those earnings is also *inviolable* and has become property of the laborer, not the government. IRS tax codes and state tax codes do not have the power to override the Supreme Law of the Land. The overwhelming taxation has become insurmountable with layers of extortion based off of what has been defined as *income* now characterized and interpreted as labor, capital, and principal. No reversal or formal modification that redefines the word *income* exists in the U.S. Constitution. What is now evident, is that government can only collect taxes on duties, imposts, and excises not on labor, capital, or even principal.

The Supreme Court is crystal clear on the subject of what can and cannot be taxed when it ruled in **Eisner v. Macomber** (1920), 252 U.S. 189 that

> "**Income** may be **defined** as the **gain** derived **from capital**." (Emphasis mine).

In order for there to be gain, one must INVEST capital to derive gain from capital. Gain is income when money makes money. Government, controlled by the Federal Reserve and IRS tax frauds, can only tax a person's gain. Though gain is comparable in form to capital and principal neither are to be confused with income.

The pink elephant in the room begs the question, why are the People paying out egregious taxes that government has no entitlement to? The answer is that we have all been conditioned into voluntarily waiving our 5th Amendment right by placing our inscribed signatures upon contracts we know as IRS tax forms. From a personal perspective, the federal government doesn't really need to tax the People directly for anything when they print money at will, but a deliberate government exploit of counterfeiting would be too brazen of an act and would wake up even the most languorous of people. The rabbit hole goes much deeper and doesn't end here. These three topics will continue to have a stronghold on other factors that keep the People under the government which was not the intention of our Forefathers who created the framework of the U.S. Constitution.

CHAPTER 8

CIVIL RIGHTS vs. UNALIENABLE RIGHTS

Whenever a political candidate or incumbent talks about the word democracy, it tells me they have no clue about American governance or policy making. It is extremely frustrating to hear because the United States of America is not a democracy, it is a REPUBLIC. Those two words are not interchangeable. They have entirely different meanings. In fact, America's Forefathers loathed any form of democracy. James Madison wrote in the Federalist Papers No. 10 that

> "Hence it is that **democracies** have ever been **spectacles of turbulence and contention**; have ever been **found incompatible** with personal security or the rights of property; and in general, have been as short in their lives as they have been **violent** in their **deaths** … A **republic**, by which I mean a government in which a scheme of representation takes place, opens a different prospect and promises the cure for which we are seeking." (Emphasis mine).

Alexander Hamilton debated during the Federal Convention of 1787 that

"We are now forming a **republican government**. Real liberty is neither found in **despotism** or the **extremes of democracy**, but in moderate governments ... But if we incline too much to **democracy**, we shall soon **shoot into a monarchy**." (Emphasis mine).

John Adams wrote in 1814 in a letter to John Taylor,

"Remember, **democracy** never lasts long. It soon **wastes, exhausts,** and **murders** itself. There is never a democracy that did not commit **suicide**." (Emphasis mine).

Fischer Ames, a forgotten Forefather, said,

"A **democracy** is **a volcano** which conceals the **fiery** materials of its own destruction. These will produce an eruption and carry **desolation** in their way. The known propensity of a democracy is to **licentiousness** (*sexual immorality*) which the ambitious call, and ignorant believe to be liberty." (Emphasis mine).

America's Forebearers were ahead of their time. Their eerily descriptive words concerning democracy such as turbulence, contention, despotism, and licentiousness could not paint a more perfect mural of the current unscrupulous and knavish activities infiltrating our present-day American government. The Framers of our government wanted to ensure that the United States would not fall prey to the bewitching and deceptive nature of a democracy. This fervor led them to write and guarantee it into the U.S. Constitution in Article IV. Sec. 4 which reads,

> "The United States **shall guarantee** to every State in this Union a **Republican Form** of **government**." (Emphasis mine).

The word democracy does not exist in the Declaration of Independence, Bill of Rights, or anywhere else in the U.S. Constitution. My recommendation is to remove it from your vocabulary! If you find yourself listening to a candidate or an incumbent uttering the word democracy or democratic society, do not vote for them or cease in re-electing them.

The term democracy is purposely being orchestrated to overshadow the word REPUBLIC because it resembles the name of the Republican political party and the word democracy sounds similar to the name of the opposing political party, the Democrats. The use of the word democracy changes the perception of an ill-informed voter to vote according to the type of government they believe embodies America and then they cast their vote to what sounds most familiar. It's a simple subliminal method that is extremely effective. Knowledge is key when dealing with rotten representation. The People must be more fundamentally astute with the Supreme Law of the Land in order to not become misled by candidates pining for votes. You should not hand off the responsibility to be informed on the nature and foundation of your government's framework for the purpose of not disrupting your decadents. A lack of involvement provides opportunity for the disingenuous to proliferate.

Odious servants of the People strive to permeate civil rights over unalienable rights. Civil rights are nothing but immunity and privileges given out by government under eligibility through the exploitation of the *Contract Clause*. According to the ABA, unalienable rights can be waived unknown by the endorser when they bind themselves to a contract. Civil rights create a second-tier status that perpetuates the falsity of the People being under the rule of government. If government gives you a right, don't accept it because it is already yours. Rights are not theirs to give. If you accept it, you can be sure the government will weaponize it against you.

According to the Declaration of Independence, unalienable rights are natural God-given rights that cannot be bought, sold, transferred, given away, waived, or contracted away known or unknown by the People. Unalienable rights monumentally solidify the People's status to remain above government. This was granted by the Creator at all times. It is by no coincidence that civil rights are a mere repackaging and demoralization of what the People have already been bestowed with by *Nature and of Nature's God*.

Activists argue that civil rights guarantee equal social opportunities and protection under the law regardless of race, religion, or other characteristics. A guarantee to equal opportunity is a person's own pursuit of happiness. Protection under the law is a cheap imitation to the protection endowed by the Creator with the unalienable right to liberty which is the very antithesis to false imprisonment and subjugation trickery. Protection regardless of race, religion, or other characteristics befuddles the self-evident truths that ALL men are created equal as stated in the Declaration of Independence,

> "We hold these **Truths** to be **self-evident**, that **all Men are created equal**, that they are **endowed** by

their Creator with certain **Unalienable Rights**, that among these are **Life**, **Liberty**, and the **Pursuit of Happiness** - That to secure these Rights, Governments are instituted among Men, deriving their just Powers from the Consent of the Governed." (Emphasis mine).

Civil rights are a counterfeit to the endowment unalienable rights yield that are already gifted to mankind by the Creator. As a political candidate, I stand firmly that I will never fight in favor of spurious liberties. My fight is to protect and preserve that which is naturally God-given. ALL candidates and representatives should have a similar ambition because that is the foundation of what our government is built on.

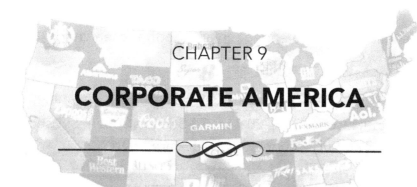

CHAPTER 9

CORPORATE AMERICA

Since the United States is illegally operating under a corporational status, the ABA falsely legitimizes that the People can sign away their rights voluntarily which creates an illusion over the People that they fall under business doctrine. Egregiously, all of the states within America consequently function as corporations and they no longer perform as nation states.

A nation state is your nationality. The state and the nation are identical, but the country does not have a predominant ethnic faction. Therefore, the state that you live in is your nation. If you live in California, your nationality is a Californian. If you live in Texas, your nationality is a Texan and so forth for each of the states within America. In general, your nation state is a sovereign province or territory considered to be a dominated terrain by an assimilated multicultural community of bodies. All of these nation states have agreed to unify and create a country the People now call America.

When I speak about the United States functioning as a corporation, I end up with half a crowd shaking their fists that such provocation has to be a fabrication and the other half of the room simply staring at me like deer in the headlights wondering why that is such an awful notion. Again, I encourage everyone to be vigilant and test the spirit of information when presented to you. Use the critical thinking the main stream media tells you not to engage in and do the research for yourself.

Proof that Corporate America is not a myth is found in the United States Code; Title 28 (U.S.C.) Section 3002 – Subsection 15 & 15A. The Subsection 15 and 15A are titled

15: *United States Means*

15A: *Federal Corporation.*

The threat behind any corporation is in their primary purpose. The primary purpose of all corporations is to achieve PROFIT. At some point in time, every business will encounter a plateau. It doesn't matter if it's caused by healthy competition, bad reputation, work force dissatisfaction, poor customer service, reduction in the quality of a product, or that the open market no longer has a need for a particular merchandise or type of service. Unfortunately, corporatists are avaricious. Their appetites are insatiable to increase their revenue year-over-year. This has led C.E.O.'s to become masters in the art of swaying government representatives with erotic lucre. Their handling shrewdly manipulates commercial activities in their favor through legislative treachery that the People are bondage to and later taxed in order to settle their crooked debts.

The fraudulent bondage placed over the People will never accomplish the corporatists desired profit margin if the endorser's jurisdictional status remains above government. This is the main reason why the exploitation of the *Contract Clause* is so important. Unalienable rights block Corporate American corruption because they can only function through businesses and business law. Their fictional authority hides within the twisting of linguistical canons that take advantage of the *Contract Clause* because they cannot operate under the Laws of Nature that which is God-given and the absolute power of His Law. More directly, Corporate America needs Common Law wholly abolished to legitimize their horrid subjugation.

The Declaration of Independence says,

> "When in the Course of human Events, it becomes necessary for one People to dissolve the Political Bands which have connected them with another, and to assume among the Powers of the Earth, the separate and equal Station to which **the Laws of Nature and of Nature's God entitle them**, a decent Respect to the Opinions of Mankind requires that they should declare the causes which impel them to the Separation.
>
> We hold these Truths to be self-evident, that all Men are created equal, that **they are endowed by their Creator** with certain **unalienable Rights**, that **among** these are **Life, Liberty, and the Pursuit of Happiness**——That to secure these Rights, Governments are instituted among Men, deriving their just Powers from the Consent of the Governed." (Emphasis mine).

Government has no authority over *nature* and they are tenaciously resistant to that word because of the entitlement it bestows. Government cannot create more land, water, or air because those are part of the natural occurring environment. The *Consent of the Governed* only permits government to regulate what nature already provides and can only be used for the good of the community that does not interfere with the behavior of the People. Unalienable rights are the BEHAVIORS that the Laws of Nature innately direct a man to live life in freedom and finding their place in the world. These rights are a gift, an endowment, from God. His Law conceived symbiosis between nature and man. More accurately, when we talk about nature, we are talking about the Absolute Being and man's connection to the Creator.

California State Constitution in Article I. Sec. 1 states,

> "**All people** are by **nature free** and **independent** and have **inalienable rights**. Among these are enjoying and **defending** life and liberty, acquiring, possessing, and protecting property, and pursuing and obtaining safety, happiness, and **privacy**." (Emphasis mine).

The word *nature* keeps coming up. The significance of its removal cannot be overlooked. It will become plain as day that its elimination is the single most audacious and atrocious attack upon any people by their own government in order to implement a monstrous and wicked level of enslavement. A sovereign to thralldom has always been the ultimate design.

CHAPTER 10

RUNNING THE STATE LIKE A BUSINESS

Candidates that spout out the nonsense that we should run the state like a business are the epidemy of ignorance. They propagate democracy and not America's Constitutional Republic. It is apparent that they have never studied the U.S. Constitution nor have they ever studied, let alone read, their own state's constitution. Truthfully, most candidates don't even know a state constitution exists.

Several people have made the correlation that being an illustrious business owner and a solid government executive are connected. They are not. Being a previous small business owner or a major corporate C.E.O. prior to holding office does not mean you should run the state the way you ran a business. Good governance deals in protecting and securing the rights of the People and is never to be eroded by illustrious charlatans. When a politician runs the state like a business, they are in fact acting against the body of the state by engaging in profiteering which is achieved through business transactions.

Remember, the U.S. Constitution is the definition to the limitation of powers. It does not grant them mastery meaning the ability to expand vested authority over their constituents. Your representatives are not permitted to force commercial activities that would financially benefit any conglomerate or purposely inflate the state budget without seeking the People's consultation first. Nor are they permitted to endorse enterprise pacts that would force a guaranteed profit margin for themselves through legislation that would leverage, corner, or impinge upon an open, fair, and free market.

In the midst of the Covid-19 Lockdowns, Governor Gavin Newsom signed into law AB 1084 also known as the Gender-Neutral Retail Department Act. The language of this bill reads,

> "This bill would require a retail department store that is physically located in California that has a total of 500 or more employees across all California retail department store locations that sells childcare items or toys to maintain a gender neutral section or area, to be labeled at the discretion of the retailer, in which a reasonable selection of the items and toys for children that it sells shall be displayed, regardless of whether they have been traditionally marketed for either girls or for boys."

The new legislation was introduced by lawmakers Cristina Garcia and Evan Low. Assemblyman Low told AP News and Today that he was inspired to write the bill by the 10-year-old daughter of one of his staffers. Assemblyman Evan Low stated on October 11, 2021, in one of Today's on-line articles,

> "My hope is this bill **encourages** more businesses across California and the U.S. to avoid reinforcing harmful and outdated stereotypes." (Emphasis mine).

It's odd to read Assemblyman Low's comment about encouragement, when stores who fail to meet the requirements by January 1, 2024, face a $250 fine for their first offense and a $500 fine for each subsequent violation. These fines are not encouragement, they are threats and they force behavioral commerce. Government only has the authority to regulate commercial activity that does not cross the line of monopolies, illicit activities, or controlled behavior. AB 1084 attempts to steer individuals to accept gender neutrality that disrupts that which is of *Nature and of Nature's God* by way of commerce. This bill corners the market rather than allowing the free market to do what it does best, to be free and unmolested by government interference. If government can deceptively convince the People into pledging their state like a business, the government can then defy the Laws of Nature and enslave a free people into an endless deficit.

State assembly and senate members will have their lawyers draft or by and large receive *model bills* from corporatist attorneys. If passed, these bills will extort the People into having to make good on payment for whatever deal is drafted through taxation even if the bill is made in bad faith. These bills are usually a plug and play where the language gets shifted around. The framework is always geared towards favouring whatever horde seeks out your local legislator to remove potential restrictions on an association aiming to increase their revenue. This is where exuberant amounts of campaign donations come onto the scene. A pay to play, if you will. For instance,

Californian voters were propositioned for the development of a bullet train that would connect the north and the south effectively propelling and rejuvenating California's economic status as an industrial powerhouse. The People permitted for the sale of 9 billion dollars in state bonds for a high-speed railway segment connecting Los Angeles and San Francisco to be completed by 2020. These are two heavily populated and popular cities in California. It was understandable why the People supported and thought this to be a good idea when it was proposed by state officials. However, years later, California has yet to construct a single mile of track. 5 billion dollars have been spent with nothing to show for it except for a few eyesores of partially connected pillars and flats and maybe a few cranes and steel beams that lay by the wayside. California law makers are currently scrambling to shorten the promised 500 miles of high-speed rail line down to 172 miles in order to prove their proof of concept will work state wide. They hope to propose another segment to be completed from Merced to Bakersfield by 2030 which will add another 20-billion-dollar price tag toward the already approved 9-billion-dollar expense. Sadly, the People have little appetite to travel from those two locations mainly due to the fact that those are not bustling areas in California for tourist attractions, vacation destinations, or locations with a high demand for a larger workforce. More money and an extended completion date would be needed to conclude an already monumental fiasco. This is why it has been dubbed, "California's Bullet Train to Nowhere."

This is a prime display of government profiteering. It is a purposeful mismanagement of taxpayer funds with zero liability. It's a beautiful illustration of government deals being made in bad faith that fatten engineers, labor unions, contractors of all sorts, and bureaucrats bank accounts with no accountability. Because of the purposed promise, under CONTRACT, the People have to make good on a profit margin that was drafted behind closed doors irrelevant that the bullet train was probably never truly intended to be completed in the first place. The forging of the rail alone goes against all things green and their climate change push. This is another reason government keeps kicking the can down the road on this project. It is a pinpointed example of an exploitation of the *Contract Clause* bartered through commercial accords and tied to an assembly bill or senate bill ultimately intended to create excess reserves. The funds are then appropriated to state agencies, commissions, and boards that have been deliberately siloed to prevent public oversight committees from tracking expenditures and disbursement for culpability.

California is nearing a deficit of $73 billion at the writing of this book. It is the biggest financial deficit in state history. California's current annual budget tops $300 billion. It is the largest budget of any state. Just as California is run like a business, the federal government also runs the nation like a business that bribes, threatens, or dexterously badgers states to engage in similar ways in any area of industry that is of particular interest at the time. This is evident with the pharmaceutical industry. President Ronald Regan, former Governor of California (1967–1975) and once a Democrat turned Republican, violated his oath and signed into law the Vaccine Injury Act of 1986. This was one of the most heinous deeds any president could have enacted against their own people. This business deal gave immunity to the pharmaceutical companies and the manufacturers. The Act provided little reason for Big Pharma to prove efficacy behind their concoctions. The Congress created a trust that the taxpayers were bilked to paying into for future claims of injury against these so-called preventive measures. When claims of damages were filed, the judicial branch assembled a vaccine injury court called the Office of Special Masters. This office

91

would determine the severity of the affliction and would arbitrate if financial compensation was warranted up to a maximum amount of $250,000. This eliminated manufacturing incentive to prove efficacy behind present and future pharmaceutical products. Government representatives provided guaranteed contracts with Big Pharma to produce drugs and vaccines to which the taxpayers would have to meet the profit margin via your signed IRS tax contractual forms. These same representatives are later given a backend deal through insider stock trading, campaign fundraisers, or party donation endorsements. This is the main reason why their net worth goes from an average of a $120k salary to becoming a millionaire before they walk out of office. The end result of the Vaccine Injury Act of 1986 is that if anyone in the nation is injured by a vaccine of any kind, the taxpayers get to front the bill. The People become the responsibility insurers so that the obligation of all government contracts signed on behest of the People by their adumbrative are fulfilled. Was this legal? The short answer is no, it was not legal. It violates the Equal Protection Clause under the 14th Amendment which reads,

> "…nor shall any state deprive any person of life, liberty, or property, without due process of law; nor **deny** to any person within **its** jurisdiction the **equal protection of the laws**." (Emphasis mine).

This act also violates the California State Constitution under Article I. Sec. 7(a) which states,

> "A person may not be deprived of life, liberty, or property without due process of law or **denied equal protection of the laws**." (Emphasis mine).

The injured don't have equal protection of the laws when the opposing side that caused the damages has immunity. However, there's a catch. You are technically not a living person under their contracts. You are a legal business entity living within the United States corporation. The government traps the People under civil authority the minute a new child is born in this country through the *Contract Clause*. This is why we don't actually have equal protection under the laws. All natural born sovereigns become an indentured slave by way of an unsuspecting contract and that is our birth certificate. It is the first and most important signed contract these corrupt in government demand to obtain. Although all states had birth records by 1919, it wasn't until 1930 that uniformity among them was adopted and not until 1946 when the National Office of Vital Statistics took over. The national birth certificates are attached to a third-party state approved surety bond company who hands the certificates off for monetary gain to the Federal Reserve. The Federal Reserve turns that surety bond into an American Bond and sells those bonds to other countries that the People are duped into paying off. It becomes a tale of freedom to captivity.

At first, I didn't believe this to be true. So, I decided to test out the information and take my own Californian birth certificate and physically inspect the document. Low and behold down on the bottom left corner, the certificate says, "PACIFIC BANCNOTE CO. NBN CO." I was curious, what is a bancnote? A bancnote is a money bill or form of currency that one party can use to pay another party. I later discovered that the Federal Reserve Bank is the only business that can print bancnotes for money. It suddenly dawned on me that no one has ownership of their original birth certificate.

Upon further inspection of my own certificate, there were very small tiny little dots barely noticeable to the naked eye stamped all up and down in rows across the document. These dots were actually letters spelling the word *void*. Now it made sense why the Federal Reserve can print bancnotes for money. Parents sign the Vital Statistics census document just days after their child is born in a hospital. In doing so, they've allowed vulturing surety bond companies and the private central banks to sell your child's future earnings. Parents only get a certified copy of the original birth certificate which is why it is voided.

My research didn't end there. Under a high-resolution camera, you can see several intertwined circles that overlap with each other layered over the tiny dots that say *void*. On top and inside the curvature of the circles are the letters SEL CROAIN UIESAE OPRTO. Some have claimed that this is an older form of Latin. Others have stated that it is classic Aramaic. Sadly, there was nothing I could discover that could confirm either claim. So, I prayed on it. It had to mean something. Why else were those letters there? Remember how the rules of engagement require that they, Satan and the *sons of disobedience*, have to tell you their plan. A few weeks later I was still continuing to pray over what this could mean and it came to me that those letters might be an anagram. I spent a few days rearranging every letter to try to form a coherent sentence. I was able to find a possible anagram for SEL CROAIN UIESAE OPRTO. The anagram is, OUR LIES ARE SET IN A COOP. A coop is a prison, jail, small enclosure, cage, or vault...like a bank vault. But COOP can also be a CO'OP. Cambridge Dictionary defines Co'op as an "organization, business...that is owned and manage by a group of people who also work in it."

The truth was revealed through my research and the Holy Spirit's guidance that we are indeed enslaved by our birth certificates. Though we've been bound to this contract, all contracts can be revoked or halted from ever being renewed by the one tethered to it. Because many people have become aware that they can repeal their bondage and they have documented the proof of their success, the tainted stewards of the People have set their aims on a more permanent means of subjugation to thwart any possible civil rescindment.

CHAPTER 11

CBDC & THE MARK OF THE BEAST

1 Timothy Chp.6 v.10 (KJV) says,

"For the **love** of **money** is the **root of all evil**."
(Emphasis mine).

Many misinterpret this verse. It is not money that is the root of all evil. It is the *love* of money that is the root of all evil. I am often asked if I believe the American government will implement a Central Bank Digital Currency (CBDC). I, without a shadow of a doubt, believe one will soon be implemented because I believe it is also biblically prophetic.

CBDC is tied to the exploitation of the *Contract Clause* from the U.S. Constitution's Article I. Sec. 10 with the omission of *voluntary servitude* that was left out of the 13th Amendment and by the solidification of the 16th Amendment which contrived debt bondage that the People were never meant to settle. At the time of the writing of this book, the United States National Debt Clock is at 34 trillion dollars. More sinisterly, CBDC will be infused into blockchain technology that mirrors Bitcoin and all other cryptocurrency type blockchains. It will virtually be un-hackable. It will also most likely be connected to an A.I. that is government controlled and nevermore will the free markets be free. Through my research there is a strong indication that CBDC will literally be tied to everyone's accumulated currency and medical health records that will be controlled by the central banks and health organizations in the most malevolent and ominous way in order for it to function properly.

Keep in mind, the corrupt in government have to tell you before they do anything due to the rules of engagement. The following relatively recent timeline of events given out by the U.S. Treasury and the current Federal Reserve Bank Chairman proves how emboldened they are. On November 20, 2019, French Hill News wrote,

> "The U.S. Federal Reserve is **eyeing development** of its own digital currency; Fed. Chairman Jerome Powell has said in a letter to federal lawmakers." (Emphasis mine).

On September 22, 2021, Market Screener/Reuters said,

> "**The Federal Reserve** will 'soon' release research **examining** the **costs** and **benefits** of a central bank digital currency, or CBDC, Fed. Chairman Jerome Powell said in a central bank policy meeting." (Emphasis mine).

At the Federal Reserve Inaugural Conference on June 06, 2022,

> "The Federal Reserve is examining whether a U.S. Central Bank Digital Currency (CBDC) would **improve** on an already safe and efficient domestic payment system and **maintain** the **dollar's international standing,** Fed. Chairman Jerome Powell announced." (Emphasis mine).

If I put those emphasized words into a sentence, they are saying **the Federal Reserve** is **examining costs and benefits** that **would improve** and **maintain** the **dollar's international standing.** These private bank shareholders, who control the world's governments, are telling you what they are doing every step of the way because they are the *sons of disobedience.*

Insider News wrote on March 02, 2023, that

> "The U.S. Treasury just gave the strongest indication yet that the U.S. **will** get a digital dollar...Nellie Liang, Under Secretary for domestic finance at the Treasury, said, '...the technological development of a CBDC **is UNDERWAY.**'" (Emphasis mine).

Furthermore, on March 09, 2023, the American Presidency Project was signed as

> "Executive Order 14067: Ensuring Responsibility Development of Digital Assets. Sec. 4 (a) (iii) A United States CBDC that is interoperable with CBDCs issued by other monetary authorities could facilitate faster and lower-cost cross-border payments and potentially boost economic growth, support the **continued centrality** of the United States within the international financial system...A Report shall be coordinated...to the extent to which foreign CBDC's could displace existing currencies and alter the payment system in ways that could undermine U.S. financial centrability..." (Emphasis mine).

The chosen words and phrases like *will*, *is underway*, and *continued centrality* paints the confirmation that America and the rest of the world will eventually be forced to use digital currency and maybe even adopt a social credit score system like China. Some would argue that this is not such a bad idea. CBDC promotes ease of use, minimization of theft, loss, or mishandling of exchanges, but that's the point. CBDC is designed to create a singular and terminal leverage over every person across every continent. Blockchain has the ability to keep clear, concise, and near perfect record of world economic transactions on a massive scale. In my opinion, it will be and is a part of the beast system that we read about in Revelation Chp.13 v.16-17 (KJV),

> "And he causeth **all**, both **small** and **great**, **rich** and **poor**, **free** and **bond**, to receive a mark **in** their **right hand**, or **in** their **foreheads**: And that no man might buy or sell, **save he** that had the **mark**, or the **name** of the beast, or the **number** of his name." (Emphasis mine).

This verse lists out the primary types of status *all* persons fall under. You are either small or great which can be translated to mean powerful or weak. You are rich or poor and are either free or bond. Bond means a forced servitude of some kind by debt bondage or imprisonment. The verse states that "no man might buy or sell." At present, there are several ways people can *buy*. It can be done by paper cash, credit cards, commodities like gold and silver, digital cryptocurrencies, stock trading, and good ol' fashion bartering of hard assets and or natural resources to name a few. We know that anything can technically be *sold* whether it's a service or a product. Providing and seeking livelihood is a right. Technically, the U.S. Constitution doesn't allow government to impinge upon your right to life. Government can regulate the market to prevent an oligopoly, but it can't force it to go in any one direction as previously discussed. It also cannot stop it unless a damage to another's right to life, liberty, or the pursuit of happiness causes injury. In order for anyone to be involved in commercial activities of any kind, city or state permits and licensing fees need to be filed and purchased. We are now back to buying, but buying from government if we want to sell anything. The government bad actors have become the permission givers to that which is unalienable.

When we look at the phrase, "save he," God is simply saying no one is going to be able to save themselves if they have one of the three identifying impressions. Let me say that again. There are three identifying types of imprints that will penetrate *in* their right hand or *in* their forehead. It will either be 1) the mark, 2) the name of the beast, or 3) the number of his name. It becomes evident and no longer theory that the mark of the beast will be biometric and will require an invasive medical procedure of some kind. This procedure could be like an inoculation which is a type of medical procedure and could become the means of placing something *in* a forehead or hand to implement the beast's mark.

I have been asked on several occasions, why the CBDC would be correlated to one's individual health record? How does this corrupt Nature's God? Why does any of this matter when America's constitution protects the rights of the People endowed by the Creator? The answer is threefold. First, the only way to corrupt Nature's God meaning to remove God is by corrupting His image. Second, in order for Satan to corrupt His image, the image can no longer be in the likeness of the Creator. And third, endowment must be eliminated to bestialize slavery into looking like freedom. None of this can be achieved without government deception.

This brings us back to the necessity of a birth certificate. The word slave is defined by the American Heritage Dictionary of the English Language, 5th Edition as,

> "One who is owned as **PROPERTY**, subservient and controlled by another and or **subject** to **specific influence**." (Emphasis mine).

The courts hold, in several cases, that a Transferee who uses fraud such as *legal fraudulent concealment* to obtain the transfer of property is a Constructive Trustee. Government is the Constructive Trustee when it comes to our birth certificate and this is why our current representatives and their puppet masters went one step further and used the Wuhan/Covid-19 pandemic as their means to establish a more stable confinement into feudalism.

The birth certificate is an agreed upon voluntary self-subservient pact parents unknowingly make that gives up their newborn's true future financial prosperity because the Federal Reserve sells those birth certificates, labeled as American bonds, to other nations in exchange for political gain. When the time comes for those beneficiary countries to call in and sell back those bonds, Congress will draft three-to-six-thousand-page bills that no one can read in the time allotted prior to passing the bill. This prevents any argument against their ludicrous financial exactions stipulated within those legislative demands. This is why American taxpayer dollars in the billions and trillions get paid out to other countries. The agreement was made through the signing of the contract in the form of a birth certificate. Under this contract we are property subjugated to an insurmountable debt. This explains why America has sent nearly 80 billion dollars to Ukraine at present.

CHAPTER 12

CORRUPTING HIS IMAGE

When we talk about contracts, we usually think about a document that involves an inked signature. Today, a contract may involve a computer-generated signature and the press of a few buttons to sign electronic forms or documents. Regardless of which method is utilized to acquire the signature, most contracts involve a document. What we seem to always forget is the existence of INFORMAL contracts that do not require such trappings. Accepting goods and services can be sanctioned with both formal and informal contracts. Informal Contract Law renders that

> "Generally, there are a number of essential elements to the formation of an informal contract; Mutual assent; consideration or some **other validation device**; two or more contracting parties; or parties having legal capacity to contract." (Emphasis mine).

An *other validation device* is an integral key to having the Creator's endowment removed.

One of the most peculiar United States Supreme Court cases was the **Association for Molecular Pathology v. Myriad Genetics** 569 U.S. 576 that took place from 2010 to 2013. It heavily involved the Laws of Nature and human DNA. In short, Myriad

Genetics wanted to patent DNA because they could isolate certain genomes. An excerpt of the Supreme Court transcript reads,

"DNA's informational sequences and the processes that create mRNA, amino acids, and proteins occur **naturally** within cells. Scientists can, however, extract DNA from the cells using well known laboratory methods. These methods allow scientists to isolate specific segments of DNA. For instance, a particular **gene** or **part of a gene**, which can then be further studied, **manipulated**, or used. It is also possible to create DNA synthetically through processes similarly well known in the **field of genetics**. One such method begins with an **mRNA** molecule and uses the **natural** bonding properties of nucleotides to create a new, synthetic DNA molecule. The result is the inverse of the mRNA's **inverse image** of the original DNA, with one important distinction: Because the natural creation of mRNA involves splicing that removes introns, the synthetic DNA created from mRNA also contains only the exon sequences. This synthetic DNA created in the laboratory from mRNA is known as **complementary** DNA (cDNA). ... Large changes, involving the deletion, rearrangement, or duplication of hundreds or even millions of nucleotides, can result in the elimination, misplacement, or **duplication** of entire genes. Some mutations are harmless, but others can cause disease or increase the risk of disease. As a result, the **study of genetics** can lead to valuable medical breakthroughs." (Emphasis mine).

In this case, the Supreme Court ruled,

> "For the reasons that follow, we hold that a **naturally occurring DNA** segment is a product of **nature** and **not patent** eligible merely because it has been isolated, but that **cDNA** (complimentary DNA) **is patent** eligible because it is **not naturally** occurring." (Emphasis mine).

When we talk about mRNA technologies, we are talking about the field of genetics. For more than a decade, the courts have identified that mRNA inverse imagery created in a laboratory can complement natural occurring DNA. The question must be asked, how does the laboratory mingle modified-RNA (mod.RNA) to interact with natural DNA? A news brief article that interviewed Moderna's C.E.O. Stephane Bancel on August 27, 2021, confirms how mRNA technology functions. He stated,

> "At Moderna, our mission is to deliver on the promise of mRNA science to create a **new generation** of **transformative medicines** for patients. Since mRNA is an information-based platform, it works similar to **a computer's operating system**, letting researchers insert **new genetic code** from a **virus**—like adding an app—to create a **new vaccine** quickly. When Covid-19 struck, we already had nine vaccines in clinical trials using mRNA technology. The Covid-19 vaccine was our tenth. Because we had invested in building our mRNA platform, it was basically a copy and paste—inserting the **new genetic code**

into our **preexisting platform**." (Emphasis mine).

The numerous scientists that came across my campaign path during the Wuhan restrictions would snarl to everyone in the room that vaccines are one of the greatest inventions in the history of medicine and that everyone needed to trust the science. One particular doctor, proclaimed scientist, and former U.S. Army medical officer said,

> "vaccines are a tried and true validating device that have become a traditional preventive standard. They should not be feared."

I agree to some extent that he is right. However, Moderna's C.E.O Stephane Bancel's declaration causes me to begin to disagree with that statement. He told everyone that Moderna's Covid-19 vaccination was not a traditional type of vaccine and compared it to a computer operating system. He used the phrase, "a new generation of transformative medicines." Those words alone tell you that Moderna, Pfizer, and other pharmaceutical companies engaging in similar mod.RNA technologies are not utilizing the traditional preventive standards of a typical vaccine, if there ever was such a thing.

Another argument that challenges the safety and oddity of the Covid-19 vaccines involves Johnson and Johnson (J&J) that do not use the new mod.RNA technologies. My research revealed that J&J used what is called an adenovirus. I'm not going get too in-depth about the adenovirus technology, but what I will say is that an adenovirus acts as a delivery vehicle used to carry *genetic* material of lab created DNA. The genetic material used by J&J is an enclosed material surrounded by fat. That fat is generally the adenovirus. The end result is the same as the mRNA technology. These companies all use *genetic* material created in the lab to gain their desired results of the spike protein replication. What I find most pernicious that no one argues against is that we are dealing with GENETICS.

The Supreme Court was firm that geneticists were not permitted to patent DNA but are permitted to patent cDNA. The villainous plot behind the ability to patent cDNA is to INJECT laboratory mod.RNA into a host. That host can be any human, animal, or organic substance. No one in their sober mind would allow for this unless *legal fraudulent concealment* transpired which would have needed to be enacted through a Constructive Transferee like the venal in government.

The study of genetics has been in play for decades. The audacity of these geneticists and their bio-tech companies trying to patent naturally occurring environmental elements sounds ludicrous because it would be like trying to patent the ocean, but they've become emboldened by nefarious representatives authorizing their research and development by way of emoluments and legislation intertwined with unscrupulous contracts operating *wherever it's not said.*

When the Wuhan/Covid-19 pandemic took the world by storm, governments across all lands shut down the world's economy and constrained the People they swore to protect into medical tyranny. Authorities never pointed a gun to the People's head, beat them or pinned them down, nor did they drag anyone to line up at a hospital, urgent care, or medical dispensary to take the Covid-19 vaccine or the boosters. They simply cornered the market through pharmaceutical state business arrangements cinched by legislative usurpations.

If you accepted the Covid-19 vaccine, you were cunningly coerced by unprincipled bureaucracy into taking gene-therapy that was *legally* and *fraudulently* concealed and labeled as a vaccine. You now have what is called cDNA and are therefore patent eligible because you no longer have what is of *Nature and of Nature's God*. You are no longer endowed by the Creator with certain unalienable rights. Accepting the injection of your own free will was an informal contract with the patent holders so you could receive their gene-therapy. The *validating device* was the syringe you permitted the medical practitioner to prod you with.

This evil act beguiled the People to be beholden to the patent holders that created cDNA using mRNA bio-technology and adenovirus genetic-DNA technology. Why would they do this? It is because any person with this technology traveling through their veins has modified their blood. The image has been partially corrupted which corrupts the gift of having certain unalienable rights. That person is now property owned by the patent holders. Property can't own property. That human being has now become a THING and a thing that is property has NO RIGHTS! Your status, once above government, is now permanently under government control. You only have access to civil rights, if they permit you to even have them that are given out by the governing authorities. You are exempt from unalienable rights endowed by the Creator. Government officials are not going to listen to you. This is one of the core reasons why every grievance you express is falling on deaf ears. You are property and property owned has no voice.

Now let me caveat on one particular theory. Again, this is only a theory. Remember to test the information for yourself. Revelation Chp.3 v.5 (NKJV) says,

> "He who **overcomes** shall be clothed in white garments, and I will not **blot out** his **name** from the **Book of Life**; but I will confess his name before My Father and before His angels." (Emphasis mine).

This verse suggests that everyone's name is written in the Book of Life because you cannot blot out what wasn't already there. Is it theoretically conceivable that Christ believers who potentially corrupted the image by accepting the Covid-19 injection, which we now know to be genetic modification gene-therapy, are unable to be raptured? They haven't taken the actual mark yet, but they did partially corrupt the image. This corruption was necessary in order for the mark to function properly when it is required in the future.

There is no mistaking the fact that life is in the blood. Genesis Chp.4 v.9-10 (NKJV) says,

> "Then the LORD said to Cain, 'Where is Abel your brother?' He said, 'I do not know. Am I my brother's keeper?' And He (the LORD) said, 'What have you done? **The voice of** your brother's **blood cries out** to Me from **the ground.**'" (Emphasis mine).

This verse alone proves that blood matters to God and the spilling of blood speaks to God because we are made in His image. Our blood is a part of Him. The land is a part of Him. Is it plausible that if our blood becomes tainted and is no longer in the likeness of Him that the blood can no longer speak to God and quite horrifically prevent a believer from being raptured? I am not suggesting damnation for anyone who has taken the Covid-19 gene-therapy injection. I am merely hypothesizing that the rapture is a moment where not only will the dead in Christ rise to meet Jesus our Savior in the clouds, but also the living just as Enoch was taken into heaven without ever having physically died. Genesis Chp.5 v.24 (KJV) says,

> "And Enoch walked with God: and he was not; for **God took him**." (Emphasis mine).

After the tribulation and before His wrath believers in Christ who are presently alive will also be caught up. They will not endure physical death. The term *rapture* itself is not explicitly found in the Bible. It is derived from the Latin word *rapturo* and from the Greek word *harpazo* which translates to mean *caught up* or *snatched away*. 1 Thessalonians Chp.4 v.16-17 (NKJV) which says,

> "For the Lord Himself will descend from heaven with a shout, with the voice of an archangel, and with the trumpet of God. And the dead in Christ will rise first. Then we who are alive and remain shall be **caught up** together with them in the clouds to meet the Lord in the air. And thus, we shall always be with the Lord." (Emphasis mine).

When we speak about human DNA found in the blood, Revelation Chp.6 v.9-11 (KJV) says,

> "And when he had opened the fifth seal, I saw

under the altar the souls of them that **were slain
for the word of God**, and **for the testimony** which
they held: and they cried with a loud voice,
saying, How long, O Lord, holy and true, dost
thou not judge and **avenge our blood** on them
that dwell on the earth? And white robes were
given unto every one of them; and it was said
unto them, that they should rest yet for a little
season, until **their fellow servants** also and **their
brethren**, that **should be killed as
they** *were*, should be **fulfilled**." (Emphasis mine).

These verses speak of those martyred, *slain,* during the
tribulation for their belief in Jesus and the testimony which they
held. These martyrs who trust in the gospel's call for all to
repent and believe will continue to sound the alarm with what
they see during the tribulation. Are they the Christ believers left
behind because they tainted their blood? The Antichrist and his
followers will not tolerate their evangelism and will kill them by
beheadings. All of these martyrs are people who were alive
before the rapture, but maybe they are the believers who were
unable to be raptured because they are clearly giving testimony
and preaching the gospel. Therefore, there seems to be an
opportunity for them to prove their worthiness in Christ after
the rapture because the spilling of their blood acts as a
filtration process and the cries of their blood will be heard once
again from the ground as Abel's blood cried out when Cain
killed Abel. These believers are potentially those "who
overcome" that are mentioned in Revelation Chp.3 v.5. I
emphasize again, this is only a theory. One that I hope to be
wrong about, but one that requires further scrutiny and
investigation. We need to be willing to accept hard truths in
order to discover His truth. Our salvation depends on it.

CHAPTER 13

HISTORY REPEATING

We've all heard the old saying that history tends to repeat itself. In fact, I remember my high school teachers and military instructors preaching that if we don't learn from the past, people will be doomed to echo those same mistakes. The military was exceptionally staunch about raising the bar every time we executed our duties because the manuals and training guides that we needed to live and breathe by were written and performed by sweat, blood, and tears. Many service members were either seriously injured from a mishap or a fatality occurred during a drill or live operation leading to the establishment of the policies and protocols in those manuals and guides. My Navy training repeatedly hammered down learning from the past and getting it right the first time because lives depended on it.

This cautioning about learning from history is something that's been around for centuries. It is not surprising that it's written in the Bible in Ecclesiastes Chp.1 v.9 (NIV) which says,

> "What has been will be again, and what has been done will be done again; there is **nothing new under the sun.**" (Emphasis mine).

It's not difficult to understand what the Bible is talking about when referring to "nothing new under the sun." We need to be incredibly astute when horrors of the past creep their heads out and disguise themselves to be something different than they are because they've been mischievously wrapped up in a new package. History is repeating itself because corrupting His image goes back to the very beginning in the Bible with Adam and Eve.

The serpent's first attempt in corrupting the image was to confound the laws given to Adam set forth by God. In a very uncomplicated manner, Adam and Eve were instructed by God not to eat from the tree of knowledge of good and evil. Genesis Chp.2 v.15-17 (NIV) says,

> "The LORD God took the man and put him in the Garden of Eden to work it and take care of it. And the LORD God **commanded** the man, 'You are free to eat from any tree in the garden; but **you must not eat** from **the tree of the knowledge of good and evil**, for when you eat from it you will certainly **die**.'" (Emphasis mine).

This seems like a simple law to abide by because the consequence of engaging in disobedience and transgressing against the Creator was severe. It would bring death. Sadly, both Adam and Eve ignored His law. It was a law that would have prevented their physical death.

In Genesis Chp.3 v.11 (KJV) God says,

> "**Who told thee** that thou wast naked? Hast thou eaten of the tree, whereof I **commanded** thee that thou shouldest not eat?" (Emphasis mine).

116

According to the American Heritage Dictionary of the English Language, 5th Edition, to *command* means to have *complete authority over* and or *rule*. Because God is the living Word, author of ALL, when He speaks to instruct or chasten His word is law.

Interestingly enough, Lucifer does not make the attempt to engage in trickery with Adam, but instead seeks out his wife, Eve. Why Eve? This is truly never explained in the Bible. Through my own research, I deduce that it is because Eve was created from Adam. As a being created from Adam, Eve would have in a sense been further removed from God. Eve was not created the same way Adam was. Woman was made from Man, for Man, and named by Man as Genesis Chp.2 v.18-23 (NIV) states,

> "The LORD God said, 'It is not good for the man to be **alone**. I will make a **helper** suitable **for him**'…But for Adam no suitable helper was found. So, the LORD God caused the man to fall into a deep sleep; and while he was sleeping, he took one of the man's ribs and then closed up the place with flesh. Then the LORD God made a **woman from** the rib he had taken out of the **man**, and he brought her to the man. The man said, 'This is now bone of my bones and flesh of my flesh; she shall be **called** 'woman,' for she was taken out of man.'" (Emphasis mine).

Another possibility for why Satan would have attempted to manipulate Eve was because she was a woman. Since she was female, she was able to birth a human child and one future baby would be born generations later who was to be called

Emmanuel. If the serpent could corrupt the woman, then being fruitful and multiplying would end which was God's will for the masterpiece He made in His image as we are called in Ephesians Chp.2 v.10 (NLT) which says,

> "For we are God's **masterpiece**. He has created us anew in Christ Jesus, so we can do the good things he planned for us long ago." (Emphasis mine).

Being fruitful and multiplying is first mentioned by God to Noah and his sons in Genesis Chp.9 v.1 (NKJV) which says,

> "So God blessed Noah and his sons, and said to them: 'Be **fruitful** and **multiply**, and fill the earth.'" (Emphasis mine).

The serpent was also not a simple, little creature slithering around the tree branches, but rather something more. Whenever we want to have a greater understanding of the context of a verse, we must always go back to the source. In this case, the source would be the original language that the Bible was written in. The relaying of events surrounding the fall of man begins in the book of Genesis found in the Old Testament which was written in Hebrew. We must also take into account that God's words always have more than one meaning or purpose behind them. Let's look at the Hebrew word used in Scripture for *snake* or *serpent*, *Nachash*. *Nachash* is also used to describe *hissing*. There are debates whether or not *nachash* could also mean *bronze* or *shinning*. The debate stems from its use in Daniel Chp.10 v.6 (NIV) which reads,

"His body was like topaz, his face like lightning, his eyes like flaming torches, his arms and legs like the **gleam** of burnished **bronze** (Nachash), and his voice like the sound of a multitude." (Emphasis mine).

To dismiss one meaning of a word for the sake of the other, I believe does a disservice to His intention in choosing the word and impacts the context of the verse. Instead, all three meanings can and should be used.

Genesis Chp.3 v.14 (NET) says,

"The LORD God said to the serpent, 'Because you have done this, cursed are you **above all** the **cattle** and **all** the living creatures of the field! On your belly you will **crawl** and **dust you will eat** all the days of your life.'"

The serpent is categorized "ABOVE ALL" livestock and living creatures of the field. Noticeably, God identifies the serpent as not just some ordinary creature hissing sweet connotations in Eve's ear. The serpent had power to be charismatic towards her. Many dismiss that a snake is already on its belly. For God to curse it again to be on its belly is nonsensical. I'm not going to get too deep into whether or not this was a literal snake, if Lucifer inhabited a snake, or if it was Lucifer himself though the Bible does clarify it was indeed Satan in the Garden. What I postulate is that the serpent was no ordinary garden snake, nor was it a human. If I use all three possible meanings behind the word *nachash*, the serpent was not on its belly but standing above all cattle and all living creatures of the field. It was scaly like a snake, whispering akin to a hissing snake, and shinning

119

similar to that of gleaming bronze. Since O' Lucifer is Son of the Morning, it might not be farfetched to say Eve was deceived by the O' Whispering Shiny Scaly One.

It would make sense that when God curses the serpent who we know to be Lucifer to eat dust all the days of his life that He is merely referring to the fact that no matter what Satan puts in his mouth, he will always taste dust. It is also possible that Lucifer did inhabit a snake and that is why his new form is no longer that of splendor, but cursed to be that of a serpent humanoid hunched over on to his belly crawling, not slithering. Snakes slither, they do not crawl.

Another possible reason why Eve was tempted and not Adam was due to the fact that Adam was the first masterpiece of God. He spent more time with God before his wife was presented to him. Disobeying God and acting immorally would be less likely to cross his mind. In Genesis Chp.3 v.13 (KJV) God asks,

> "...unto the woman, 'What is this that thou hast done?' And the woman said, 'The serpent **beguiled** me, and I did eat.'" (Emphasis mine).

Beguiled means to *attract, persuade, charm,* and *lead astray* according to the Cambridge Dictionary and Oxford Language Dictionary. This provides another framework for why the serpent chose Eve instead of Adam, she was easily manipulated. Furthermore, for her to be so easily bewitched by the serpent substantiates that Satan must have stood marvelously shining, fascinating her with captivating whispers (*nachash*) baring similar qualities of a human.

Lastly, the serpent may have chosen Eve because she was lower on the hierarchy. Adam was first and more than likely had a greater affinity not to eat from the forbidden tree, but Satan knew that Adam loved Eve and she was made for him and from him. At the very least, Adam was willing to sacrifice himself to be with Eve so she would not be alone as he had been alone in the beginning even unto his own death. Genesis Chp.3 v.6 (NIV) tells us,

> "When the woman saw that the fruit of the tree
> was good for food and pleasing to the eye, and
> also desirable for gaining wisdom, she took some
> and ate it. She also gave some to her
> husband, **who was with her**, and he ate it."
> (Emphasis mine).

Adam was with her when this all took place. Since he did not stop the seduction, he may have realized that he failed in his husbandly duty to his wife and wasn't going to let her take the punishment of death alone. This becomes a sort of love story, a similar tale to that of Romeo and Juliet.

1 Corinthians Chp.11 v.3 (ASV) says,

> "But I would have you know, that **the head** of
> every **man** is Christ; and **the head** of the **woman** is
> the man." (Emphasis mine).

This is the chain of command and is why the home structure between husband and wife is so important. There are distinct roles men and women were designed to perform. Satan needed to disrupt the home so that husband and wife or man and woman could be confused in order to confound His law.

Genesis Chp.3 v.4-5 (KJV) says,

> "And the serpent said unto the woman, Ye shall
> **not surely die**: For God doth know that in the day
> ye eat thereof, then your **eyes** shall be **opened**,
> and ye **shall be as gods, knowing good and evil**."
> (Emphasis mine).

This very calculating attempt to deceive succeeded. Satan repackages what Adam and Eve already had. He tells Eve that she will not surely die promising longevity even though God had already put the tree of life in the midst of the garden. Several biblical scholars have agreed that the tree of life was a gift to Adam and Eve so they would not physically die or age. Adam and Even already had eternity with the Creator.

When the serpent tells Eve that her eyes will be opened and they shall be like gods, he was promising wisdom. God said they could eat of any tree, the tree of life being one of them, with the exception of the tree of knowledge of good and evil as Genesis Chp.2 v.9 (NKJV) says,

> "And out of the ground the LORD God
> made **every tree** grow that is pleasant to the sight
> **and good for food**. The **tree of life** was also in the
> midst of the garden, and the tree of the
> **knowledge of good and evil**." (Emphasis mine).

The serpent continues leading Eve astray about knowing good and evil, promising a knowledge that only the gods would know. Adam and Eve already had the greatest library at their fingertips. If Adam wanted to know how the Sun was built, all he needed to do was ask God and He would have told him

122

because Adam and Eve walked with God. Genesis Chp.3 v.8 (KJV) tells us,

> "And they heard the voice of the LORD God **walking in the garden** in the cool of the day." (Emphasis mine).

The serpent merely repackaged and confounded what they were already endowed with, akin to that which is of *Nature and of Nature's God.*

The U.S. Constitution harmonizes more so with Christianity than any other faith. Even though there is no definitive proof that America's Forefathers declared Christ as their Savior, their public and personal memoirs prove they had a belief in God and were extremely familiar with the writings of the Bible. They believed that the God of the Bible governs the affairs of humanity. Again, none of our Forefathers mention Jesus as their personal Savior, but they used the teachings and lessons from the Good Book to inspire elements in the creation of the Declaration of Independence and the Constitution of the United States for America. John Adams, a Founding Father and President of the United States, stated,

> "Our Constitution was made only for a moral and religious people. It is wholly inadequate to the government of any other."

James Madison wrote that our U.S. Constitution requires

> "…sufficient virtue among men for self-government."

The *Laws of Nature and of Nature's God* involve structure, balance, and purpose. Those fundamentals have been distorted, repackaged, and handed back to the People in a way the laws were never intended to be. Present day representatives are acting in a similar fashion to the serpent. They eagerly confound the language of the laws from the original framework America's Forefathers set forth for the People of our nation.

CHAPTER 14

THE GIANTS OF THE EARTH

I'm going to take you on a short caveat in this chapter because it is necessary to provide you with a greater context for the coming chapters.

Genesis Chapter 6 lays the foundation to understanding how government corrupting that which is of *Nature's God* has always been the goal in separating man from the Creator. Satan uses government deception to achieve this separation and permanently enslave people through the kingdoms of this world.

Many of us who have studied the Bible have always been fascinated by the biblical stories of giants like that of David and Goliath of Gath. The Bible makes multiple references to the existence of giants such as Goliath's four brothers, Og King of Bashan, the Amorites, the Nephilim, the Watchers, and the sons of God who mated with the daughters of men. Many theorize that the giants of old will return. I hypothesis that the giants of old are already here and operating and controlling behind the scenes through rotten government activities.

After the fall of man in the garden of Eden, Lucifer set out to corrupt His image a second time. We read in Genesis Chp.6 v.2-4 (ASV),

"That the **sons of God** saw the daughters of men
that they were fair; and they took them wives of all
which they chose. … The **Nephilim** were in the
earth in those days, and also after that, when the
sons of God came in unto the **daughters of men**,
and they **bare children** to them: The same were
the **mighty men** that were **of old**, the **men of
renown**." (Emphasis mine).

The sons of God were indeed angels as they are referenced in
Job Chp.38. v.1-7 (ESV) which reads,

"Then the LORD answered Job out of the
whirlwind and said…'Where were you when I laid
the foundation of the earth? …When the **morning
stars** sang together and all the **sons of
God** shouted for joy?'" (Emphasis mine).

Man didn't exist when the foundation of the Earth was set. The
sons of God were there. Notice the word *sons* is plural. Adam
and Eve could not have been those referenced here because
Eve is clearly identified as female and would have been
referred to as a daughter. She and Adam or their children could
not have been the intended reference.

When we look at the phrase, "morning stars," the Bible again is
describing more than one star. There are only a few places in
the Bible where the word *morning* is used to directly describe
two very powerful heavenly hosts. They are Lucifer and Jesus.
The name Lucifer has been mistranslated in various Bible
translations to *Day Star*, but that does not reflect the phrase in
either Latin or Greek. The two words *day* and *star* are a
mistranslation of the one Greek word *phosphoros*. This comes

126

from the two Greek words *phos* meaning *light* and *phero* meaning *to bear* or *carry*. The Greek word *phosphoros* means *light-bearer* or *light-bringer*, not Day Star. The name *Lucifer* is Latin. It is the superlative translation of the Greek word *phosphoros*. Both the Greek and Latin translations support each other and are absolutely one hundred percent identical in meaning.

Lucifer is called "son of the morning" in Isaiah Chp.14 v.12 (KJV) which reads,

> "How art thou fallen from heaven, **O *Lucifer*, son of the morning!** How art thou cut down to the ground, which didst weaken the nations!" (Emphasis mine).

We read of Jesus being referred to as a "morning star" in Revelation Chp.22 v.16 (ESV) that says,

> "I, **Jesus**, have sent my angel to testify to you about these things for the churches. I am the root and the descendant of David, the bright **morning star**." (Emphasis mine).

It would stand to reason that Jesus and Lucifer are singers or the musical choir leaders that led the *sons of God* in a praise of joy to God's creational workmanship. Job Chp.38 v.7 is one scripture many biblical scholars never include when debating whether Lucifer was a musician or worship leader. It is my opinion that Lucifer and the *sons of disobedience* control the music industry that influences millions down a wretched path of sin. Ezekiel Chp.28 v.13 (NKJV) provides further verification that Lucifer was a musician. It reads,

"**You** were in **Eden**, the **garden** of God; Every precious stone was your covering: The sardius, topaz, and diamond, Beryl, onyx, and jasper, Sapphire, turquoise, and emerald with gold. The **workmanship** of your **timbrels** and **pipes** was prepared for **you** on the day **you** were created." (Emphasis mine).

Aside from God, Adam, and Eve the only other being mentioned in the Garden of Eden was the serpent who we now know is Satan and is the *you* being referenced in this verse. Timbrels and pipes are musical instruments that belonged to Lucifer which may be another reason why the Hollywood music industry performs so many devilish acts on stage during award ceremonies. Lucifer is a musician who is the *god of this world* that the performers are paying homage to.

Remember I said earlier, corrupt government operates *wherever it's not said*? During the 6 days of creation, God always used the ending phrase, "and it was so" or "it was good" as we read in Genesis Chp.1 v.4-10 (ASV),

"And God saw the light, that **it was good**…And God made the firmament, and divided the waters which were under the firmament from the waters which were above the firmament: **and it was so**…And God called the dry land Earth; and the gathering together of the waters He called Seas: and God saw that **it was good**." (Emphasis mine).

God never said, "Let the *sons of God or* angels come down unto the daughters of men to mix heavenly hosts with the flesh of the Earth and birth half-breeds." He just never said they

128

couldn't do it. Those fallen angels operated wherever it was not said.

Satan needed to corrupt His image in every sense of the word which is why the hearts of all men were evil during the time of the flood. Genesis Chp.6 v.5 (KJV) says,

> "And God saw that the wickedness of man was great in the earth, and that **every imagination** of the **thoughts of his heart** was only **evil continually.**" (Emphasis mine).

The handiwork of God's image is literally written inside our chromosomes. Lucifer unknowingly proves this through Noah's lineage. Genesis Chp.6 v.9 (KJV) reads,

> "These are the generations of Noah: Noah was a **just man** and **perfect in his generations**, and Noah **walked** with God." (Emphasis mine).

I've participated in countless discussions regarding the reason why Noah and his family were chosen by God to be spared from the flood. Most people center on Noah being righteous, the only righteous man left on earth worth saving. I believe there was more to why God spared Noah. First, Noah walked with God as Adam and Eve did when they were in the Garden of Eden. Second, God recognized Noah by his actions that they were pleasing to the Lord which is why He granted Noah the title of a "just man." Noah's title is then followed up with Noah being "perfect in his generation." This acknowledgment of Noah's genealogy proves we are talking about more than just his righteousness. If his ancestry is being referenced, then one can conclude we are predominantly addressing his human ancestry. But, in what way? The Old Testament was written in Hebrew and the phrase, "perfect in his generation" was translated from the word *tamim*. The word *tamim* is defined as "without fault or flaw, defect, or **blemish**," according to Lexicon Strong's and Hebrew Translations. The definition of *tamim* predisposes Noah to be like that of a red heifer. If we re-read Genesis Chp.6 v.9 in keeping to the proper Hebrew translation, it would read,

> "These are the generations of Noah: Noah was a just man and **without blemish**, and Noah walked with God." (Emphasis mine).

Noah genetically was a pureblood. Noah had married Enoch's daughter, *Naamah* (according to Jewish tradition). Enoch was also the first person of the Bible to be raptured according to Genesis Chp.5 v.24 (ASV) which reads,

> "…and Enoch walked with God: and **he was not**; for God **took him**." (Emphasis mine).

Enoch never physically died but entered into heaven alive. It's fair to assume that if God loved Enoch so much to let him enter into heaven alive, then his daughter, Naamah, would not have been an angel human hybrid. Therefore, Noah's three sons Ham, Shem, and Japheth must have also been purebloods. This provides more clarity as to why the flood must have taken place. It occurred because the gene pool had been corrupted. His laws written in the hearts of His image meaning the blood of men was on a path to becoming extinct. Genesis Chp.6 v.12 (ASV) tells us,

> "And God saw the earth, and, behold, it was

corrupt; **for ALL flesh** had **corrupted** their way upon the earth." (Emphasis mine).

Notice how "all flesh" not some, not a couple, not just human, but "ALL FLESH" had been corrupted with the exception of Noah and his family. The fallen angels were corrupting His image and all other flesh that was made according to its kind. It started through the perversity of sexual intercourse between heavenly hosts and humans and later opened pandora's box to the mixing of human angel hybrids with animals. Today, we would refer to this as transhumanism. Transhumanism is not new. The Bible is clear that these creatures existed as we read in Isaiah Chp.13 v.21 (KJV) which states,

> "But wild beasts of the desert shall lie there; and their houses shall be full of doleful creatures; and owls shall dwell there, and **satyrs** shall dance there." (Emphasis mine).

If you believe the Bible, then you have to believe that satyrs existed. A satyr is a half-man, half-goat known for brutal lust.

Our blood, our DNA matters to God even to this day and will play a significant role in the final days that will eventually lead to the *mark of the beast*.

I've heard sermons time and time again profess that the God of the Old Testament was an angry God and the God of the New Testament is a loving God. I would argue against that. God has shown all His love, wrath, and grace throughout the entire Bible. He wasn't willing to destroy all of his masterpiece during the flood, but rather was willing to save mankind through the lineage of the one family who kept His laws and was the most genetically pure as he had intended.

When I was eleven years old, my father told me that he had planted the seed of the Word of God in me. He said that I was approaching the age of awareness and I needed to go find my own God. If the seed was planted and rooted deep enough, I would come back to Jesus. I remember taking him up on that suggestion with eager anticipation and not for the right reasons. I set out to prove there was no God.

Not many know, but my father was an alcoholic. Growing up, I struggled with my father's painful vulgarities and abusive actions towards everyone in my family the second alcohol touched his lips while he preached to us about Jesus when he was sober. He was a bit of a Dr. Jekyll and Mr. Hyde, loving one day and vile the next. I wanted to throw it back at him that Jesus was a lie and that He didn't exist. I was hell bent on proving him wrong.

I'm an 80's kid. We were the latchkey kids, feral children who raised themselves. We are the generation that played mud football in the rain and celebrated broken bones just so we could get a cool cast and have all our friends sign it the next day at school. If you had a problem with another kid, you stepped up and said what you had to say to their face. You couldn't hide behind your iPhone, Galaxy, tablet, GPS, Google, Facebook, or YouTube profile because they didn't exist. The ability to access information available at your fingertips to become more knowledgeable didn't exist in the days of my youth. I had to put a quarter in my shoe for emergencies to use at a payphone before I got on my bike and rode down to the local public library. I had to use the Dewey Decimal System to find books on the subjects I was hoping to learn more about.

On my search to find the truth about God, I would get up early on the weekend to bike ride down to the library because I was a slow learner and needed all the time I could get in before I had to ensure I was home when the street lights came on. Remember how I said earlier that I was a terrible student and my grades were poor, but not for a lack of trying? This was the first time I was truly determined to overcome my learning curve and educate myself. Before I turned 12 in 1988, I had spent the entire summer at the library trying to find books that disproved Jesus's existence and proved that the Gospel was fabricated. I tried to find archeological material or archived articles that the flood never happened or that Babylon was just fiction. I was terrible at trying to understand half of what I came across at that time, but what my research forced me to do was reference back to parts of the Bible whenever there was a citation or remark being made regarding it. In fact, everything I kept finding was proving the Bible was based in facts and Jesus was indeed real and the Son of God.

I came to understand that the God of both the Old Testament and the New Testament were one and the same. From what I could gather at such a young age, God wanted us to show Him how much we love Him as He has shown how much He loves us. One of the most important ways of proving to God how much you love him is to put Him first, above all. When the people of the Bible didn't put God first or they defied His laws, it angered Him. That anger didn't mean He stopped loving them. Instead, I found that He would chasten them. The Nephilim creatures He destroyed by flood were not of His making, but the distortion of what Lucifer and the Watchers had done to pervert that which was made in His likeness and every flesh of its kind.

133

Undoubtedly, corrupting Nature's God through government deception has now become Lucifer's third attempt to destroy His image.

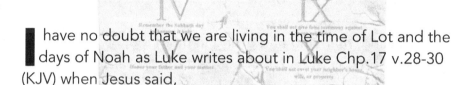

CHAPTER 15

AS IT WAS IN THE DAYS OF OLD

I have no doubt that we are living in the time of Lot and the days of Noah as Luke writes about in Luke Chp.17 v.28-30 (KJV) when Jesus said,

> "Likewise, also **as it was** in the **days of Lot**; they did eat, they drank, they bought, they sold, they planted, they builded; But the same day that Lot went out of Sodom it rained **fire** and **brimstone** from heaven, and **destroyed them all**. Even thus shall it be in the day when the **Son of man is revealed**." (Emphasis mine).

The time of Lot was a time of sexual immorality, debauchery, adulterous fornication, and child besmirchment. We read in Genesis Chapter 19 that Lot offered his two daughters as a carnal offering to appease the perverse mongrel sodomites who wanted to KNOW Lot's guests. The guests were angels of the Lord and this proves the time of Lot was an age of licentiousness. Today, the number of countless pedophiles that get caught on camera trying to lure children through the internet to meet up at a store, movie theater, park, mall, or some other apparently harmless location is astounding. These deviants are becoming more emboldened because present day laws throughout the country lean more towards protecting the criminal rather than the victims. When society fails to protect the innocent, we fail to protect virtue. When government fails to remedy a crime in order to exonerate the criminal, the innocent is avenged by merciless carnage.

We read in Mathew Chp.24. v.37-39 (ESV) that

> "For as were the days of Noah, so will be the coming of the Son of Man. For as in those days before the flood they were **eating** and **drinking, marrying** and **giving in marriage,** until the day when Noah entered the ark, and **they were unaware until** the flood came and swept them all away, so will be the coming of the Son of Man." (Emphasis mine).

When Jesus said, "as were the days of Noah" he was telling the people of the future that the final generation will not be enduring the exact same problems, but rather similar conflicts. When we compare Noah's time to present day, we find that Noah was living in a time of giants who were the "heroes of old and men of renown," according to Genesis Chp.6 v.4. Noah was dealing with physical giants who had great power in his time. Today, we have different types of giants. This last generation is dealing with Tech Giants. America is heavily deceived by power-hungry corporate industries wickedly plotting our spiritual demise. The powerful tech companies have the capacity to silence a sitting United States President. Whether you believe the 2020 Presidential election was stolen or not is irrelevant to the fact that internet media moguls controlled or silenced President Trump's ability to speak to the public while simultaneously crushing any opposition to the controlled narrative. Social media power houses influence the feelings and minds of all ages. They have the power to promote falsities as truth and the clout to dismantle conflicting speculations or evidence. They are feared for their ability to shape the court of public opinion. Tech Giants are also in reference to bio-tech pharmaceutical companies. The Bible has prophesied about their ability to consume the light of believers and lay desolate the Church as they circumvent every nation on Earth. They have a power unlike any previous generation has ever witnessed or has ever had to endure. Revelation Chp.18 v.23 (ASV) says,

> "...and the **light** of a lamp **shall shine no more** at all in thee; and the **voice** of the **bridegroom** and of the **bride** shall be heard **no more** at all in thee: for thy merchants were the **princes of the earth**; for with thy **sorcery** were **all the nations deceived**." (Emphasis mine)

Since the New Testament was written in Greek, the word *sorcery* is translated from the Greek word *pharmakeia* which is where the medical industry derives the word *pharmacy*. It would stand to reason that this is one of the primary industries Satan will use to forcefully back all of humanity into a corner.

It doesn't surprise me that the people during Noah and Lot's time were going about their day-to-day as if the evils of their world didn't plague every moment of their lives. Those people could only be unaware of the extensive immorality if they deliberately chose to ignore the signs of God and instead partook in the abominations of their obscenities. Unfortunately, many people today will miss the signs God has revealed for several reasons. They lack the understanding of what heavenly signs are, where to look for them, and why they are extremely important. They have simply forgotten to look up. God tells us in Genesis Chp.1 v.14 (ESV),

> "Let there be lights in the expanse of the heavens
> to separate the day from the night. And let them
> be for **signs** and for seasons, and for days and
> years." (Emphasis mine).

Many Christians have all heard of the blood moons and the ominous warnings they bring. Some of these blood moons have come as a dyad or a tetrad and they've landed on specific biblical festivals which we would call God's appointed times. They are often spread out over two or three years. Tetrads are extremely rare. What is even more rare are pentads, heptads, and octads. Baby Boomers, Gen X'ers, Millennials, and Gen Z are the only American generations to be given a nonad which is a series of 9 signs in the heavens. The signs have all landed on God's Holy Days beginning in 2014 and continuing through 2017. They will also be the only generations to bear witness to three Great American Eclipses. No other generation has been given so many signs from the heavens that have been profoundly ignored. The following are the dates and the biblical festivals that they have occurred on:

- April 15, 2014, a Lunar Eclipse occurred during **Passover**
- October 8, 2014, a Lunar Eclipse took place on **Sukkot**
- March 20, 2015, a Solar Eclipse happened on the **1st of Nissan**
- April 4, 2015, a Lunar Eclipse occurred during **Passover**
- September 13, 2015, a Partial Solar Eclipse took place on the **1st of Tishri**
- September 28, 2015, a Lunar Eclipse took place on **Sukkot**
- March 23, 2016, a Partial Lunar Eclipse happened during

Passover
- September 16, 2016, a Partial Lunar Eclipse occurred on **Sukkot**
- August 21, 2017, a Great American Solar Eclipse happened during **Yom Kippur (Day of Repentance)**

These signs will not end here. At the time of the writing of this book, the second Great American Eclipse known as the Ring of Fire Eclipse has just taken place as it moved across the United States on October 14, 2023, during the biblical festival of Tishri. The Ring of Fire Eclipse will proceed the third Great American Eclipse expected on April 8, 2024 by only 6 months. The third Great American Eclipse will occur during Passover. The significance of these events is that America hasn't seen such an extensive solar eclipse across the nation in over 40 years, let alone three that span over nearly 7 years. The number 7 is biblically symbolic and represents completion. We have to ask ourselves what these signs could reveal the completion of?

If we take the movement of the first and third Great American Solar Eclipses, they form the letter X. This is also the last letter of the Ancient Semitic Hebrew alphabet known as *Tav* which is an image of crossed sticks. According to Judaism, *Tav* means an *impression* or *to mark*. *Tav* also represents *truth*.

If we take the three paths created from the first Great American Solar Eclipse, the Ring of Fire Eclipse, and the third Great American Solar Eclipse which occurred in 2017, 2023, and 2024, they form the letter *El* which is the first letter of the Ancient Semitic Hebrew alphabet. The root word of *El* in Hebrew means *might, strength,* or *power*. In scripture, the meaning of the root word *El* is *god (a deity), God (true God of Israel),* or the *mighty (referring to angels or men)*.

139

The first and last letters are potentially being symbolized across the heavens over America to refer to the Alpha and the Omega. If we are to only find meaning behind the first letter *El*, then I would surmise God's message over America is that we must love the Lord God first, His law first, and seek first His kingdom. If we are to only find meaning behind the last letter, *Tav*, then I would speculate God's message over the United States is that America is marked by truth which is Jesus or that truth will be revealed. Jesus says in John Chp.14 v.6 (NIV),

> "I am the way and **the truth** and the life. No one comes to the Father except through me." (Emphasis mine).

The first and last letter also symbolize a beginning and an end. If truth, Jesus, is marking America then Jesus may be telling the people of the United States that America is living a lie, is pressured by lies, and will potentially end because of lies. This is a powerful sign that His revival will begin and it must begin with truth. Revival usual commences when a people are under tremendous conviction usually caused by deep spiritual strife or due to enduring tumultuous times. Ephesians Chp.6 v.12 (KJV) says,

> "For **we wrestle** not against flesh and blood, but **against principalities**, against powers, against the rulers of the darkness of this world, **against spiritual wickedness in high places**." (Emphasis mine).

I find it apropos that Gen Z (1997-2012) and Gen Alpha (2013-2025) are so appropriately labeled. Gen Z utilizes the last letter of the English alphabet and symbolizes the end, *Tav*. Gen

Alpha means the beginning, *El*. I do not believe there to be another generation after these two. I do not mean that these generations will not have descendants, but I doubt their offspring will see adulthood or possibly the age of awareness. I cannot speak for other countries, but in America the majority of these generations especially Gen Z which is the rifest with asininity has ignored the multitude of heavenly warnings. If our nation were to heed the warnings and repent from their evil ways, God would restore our land as we read in 2 Chronicles Chp.7 v.14 (KJV) which says,

> "If my people, which are called by my name, shall humble themselves, and pray, and seek my face, and **turn from their wicked ways**; then will I hear from heaven, and will forgive their sin, and will **heal their land**." (Emphasis mine).

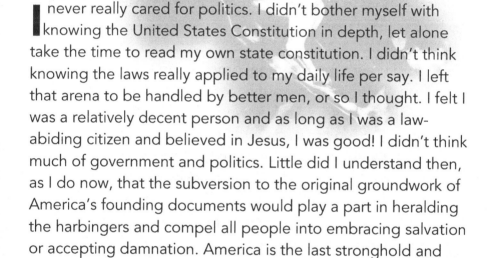

CHAPTER 16

THE FOUR HORSEMEN RIDE: THE WHITE HORSE

I never really cared for politics. I didn't bother myself with knowing the United States Constitution in depth, let alone take the time to read my own state constitution. I didn't think knowing the laws really applied to my daily life per say. I left that arena to be handled by better men, or so I thought. I felt I was a relatively decent person and as long as I was a law-abiding citizen and believed in Jesus, I was good! I didn't think much of government and politics. Little did I understand then, as I do now, that the subversion to the original groundwork of America's founding documents would play a part in heralding the harbingers and compel all people into embracing salvation or accepting damnation. America is the last stronghold and only a flickering gleam of light scarcely remains. The People today have little interest in God and the governing laws of the land they occupy. They assume they have better things to do. The truth of the matter is that the meaning and meaningfulness of our mortal walk requires us to comprehend both in order for our true purpose to take effect.

The prevailing despotism of the United States is without a doubt by design. It is structured within areas of industry that all people operate within on a routine basis. Each of those industries will subdue the strong, tire the just, bankrupt the meek, and starve the destitute. It is within these areas of enterprise that suborned government engage in their distortive nature to subvert American doctrine and it is within these enterprises that the horsemen initiate their gallop.

There is a confusion about who breaks the first four seals from the scroll in Revelation. Many Christians suggest that Lucifer is behind the atrocities the riders leave in their wake. He is not. Lucifer is merely maneuvering his armada in place at this time, like chess pieces on a board. He is ready to exploit the muddled nations in the midst of their future chaos. Revelation Chp.5 v.2-7 (ESV) reads,

> "And I saw a mighty angel proclaiming with a loud voice, 'Who is worthy to open the scroll and break its seals?'... And between the throne and the four living creatures and among the elders I **saw a Lamb** standing, as though it had been **slain**, with seven horns and with seven eyes, which are the seven spirits of God sent out into all the earth. And he went and **took the scroll** from the right hand of him who was seated on the throne." (Emphasis mine).

The Lamb is actually Jesus. Jesus is the only one in Heaven who is worthy to break open the seals. When the Lamb, Jesus, breaks open the first seal, the rider of the white horse is released. In the book of Revelation, it is the white horse that launches the first set of assaults upon the sovereigns of all nations obscuring curative means that would sustain or prolong the physical human existence. My personal research leads me to believe this encroachment is accomplished through manipulating our health!

Revelation Chp.6 v.1-2 (ESV) says,

> "Now I watched when the Lamb opened one
> of the seven seals, and I heard one of the four
> living creatures say with a voice like
> thunder, 'Come!' And I looked, and behold, a
> **white horse!** And its rider had a **bow**, and a **crown**
> was given to him, and he came out **conquering,**
> and **to conquer.**" (Emphasis mine).

The word *bow* in Greek means *toxon* or *toxikon* which is a bow and its ARROW dipped in poison. If I look at the original translation behind *crown* that word was translated from the Greek word *corona*. This white horse has the power to conquer with a poisonous armament. The weapon of choice by the rider of the white horse, in my opinion, tells me that he comes out conquering without brutal force. Instead, the rider uses a tactic only the weak would employ to subdue the strong. There is only one crown that has ever conquered the entire world without brutal force that is still engaged in subjugation to this day and that is the Corona Virus. The Wuhan/Covid-19 pandemic put fear in some of the most formidable people across all lands.

Take notice that the rider of the white horse is wearing the crown. Crowns represent ruling authorities. The damage they can yield is found in the power they hold over a multitude. However, it is the rider's chosen weapon of the bow and its arrow dipped in poison that causes the real damage. It is my belief that the bow and arrow is a representation of the Covid-19 gene-therapy/vaccine syringe. The syringe is infused with a solution delivered through a needle. This solution is the killing agent similar to poison which conquers or rather attempts to weaken and eventually vanquish all opposition slowly over time. I can only suspect that the color white was given to the rider because the area of enterprise is within the medical construct particularly the pharmaceutical and health industry. Every doctor from a variety of fields within the science and medical community are given a white lab coat upon their graduation or start of their career. Like an artist marking ownership, it is by no coincidence that the caduceus, a short staff entwined by two serpents, is the primary logo and the umbrella symbol for the entire health organization. With a more refined translation and understanding now in place, a second interpretive reading of the first seal is warranted,

> "And I looked, and behold, the **pharmaceutical medical industry!** And the **scientist** had a **poisonous syringe**, a **corona virus** was given to the **doctor**, and he came out **subduing**, and to **subdue without physical force.**" (Opinion creative, translation mine).

There is enough evidence to prove the white horse of the apocalypse will come through the pharmaceutical medical industry. Understand that not all medicine or acute medication is designed with malicious intent. However, because people are blinded by a doctor's accolades, a person's critical thinking skills often stop when they see the white lab coat. They unintentionally propagate the pharmaceutical community which becomes the perfect venue for an unsuspecting assault on the world's health industry. Everything that involves a person's health will be circumvented by every major health organization worldwide. The World Health Organization (WHO), the Center for Disease Control (CDC), the Food and Drug Administration (FDA), the National Institution of Health (NIH), The American

Medical Association (AMA), Pfizer, Moderna, and AstraZeneca are a few examples of organizations that have a level of control over the institutions of world government that Alexander the Great would be envious of.

Earlier I said that the *prince of the power of the air* will possibly intertwine CBDC with everyone's medical records and health statistics with blockchain technology. Blockchain technology requires electrical power, the world wide web (www), and lots of wireless communication towers. The major health organizations are already using blockchain technology to centralize data logs that are incorruptible and transparent. It is used to create complex codes that protect an individual's identification and medical documents, to live-stream remote patient vitals, and provide genetic information while ensuring quick transfer of information to reduce the window of time in which data can be accessed by your physician or medical team. Lucifer controls the air ways and transmission of messaging by way of the *Cloud*. This is why he is the *prince of the power of the air*.

The NIH, National Library of Medicine, and National Center for Biotechnology Information had an investigative study report written by Beverly Rubik and Robert R. Brown that was published on September 29, 2021. The report was on Wireless Communication Radiation and Covid-19. It stated there was,

> "...a statistical correlation to international communities with recently established 5G networks. In this study, we examined the peer-reviewed scientific literature on the detrimental bioeffects of Wireless Communication Radiation (WCR) and identified several mechanisms by

which WCR may have **contributed** to the COVID-19 pandemic as a **toxic** environmental **co-factor.**" (Emphasis mine).

Those co-factors were identified as,

"hypercoagulation, impaired microcirculation, hemoglobin levels exacerbating hypoxia, amplified immune system dysfunction, including immunosuppression, autoimmunity, and hyperinflammation, increase cellular oxidative stress and the production of free radicals resulting in **vascular injury** and organ damage, increase in promoting pro-inflammatory pathways and worsen **heart arrhythmias** and **cardiac disorders.**" (Emphasis mine).

Radio Frequencies (RF), WiFi, Satellite, GPS, and Bluetooth are types of wireless communication that give off ranges of radiation. The RF signals from cell phones as well as Bluetooth and WiFi are considered non-ionizing forms of radiation. That means unlike ionizing radiation from the sun or medical tests such as CT scans or x-rays, they don't carry enough energy to directly damage or alter your DNA. However, prolonged exposure can cause cancer. What the science community doesn't say out loud is that non-ionizing radiation can have measurable effects on all living organisms. It is a matter of extensive dispute as to how worrisome those effects are.

We must connect the dots. It is peculiar that the NIH would have put out a study to investigate WCR in tandem with Covid-19. I don't believe in coincidences. Remember, the *sons of disobedience* must always show their hand before they do something because that is a rule of engagement. If God reveals it, so must Satan. How they obscurely tell us their plan, is up to them. Those who have eyes to see and ears to hear, who are willing to educate themselves, and show themselves to be approved will see the revelation of their plan plain as day. 2 Timothy Chp.2 v.15 (KJV) says,

> "**Study** to **shew thyself approved** unto God, a workman that needeth not to be ashamed, rightly dividing the word of truth." (Emphasis mine).

Remember, under the *Contract Clause* government and their agencies like state health departments can also engage in *legal fraudulent concealment*. There have been several debates regarding the contents of the mod.RNA vaccine vials among doctors who have investigated them under a microscope. Many of the doctors proclaimed that the vaccines were indeed scandalous. One of the main ingredients found was a Graphene Oxide (GO) like material. GO is used by biotech companies for based applications in electronics, optics, chemistry, energy storage, and biology. Of course, when this was revealed to the public every major news media outlet, social media fact-checker, and major health organization fought to debunk what they called, "misinformation."

Under the Freedom of Information Act (FOIA), opposing scientists and medical researchers were suing the FDA to release Pfizer's documents relating to the Covid-19 vaccination and for full disclosure of their vaccine content. The FDA, on Pfizer's behalf, asked the courts that disclosure of their vaccine contents be denied until 2096. This was roughly a delay in the release of information for 75 years. Let's face the facts, nearly every generation who took or is about to take the Covid-19 vaccine and could possibly experience side-effects would be in their final retirement years or be six feet under before Pfizer's full transparency policy would take effect. As a businessman, if I create a product or a service, I should have no problem standing behind the efficacy of my product and the certainty of my service. I should be willing to welcome public scrutiny through full disclosure. Pfizer's resistance to revealing the detailed information and the FDA's argument against the disclosure proves there is a far more nefarious reason behind their request for a postponement in providing the information to the public.

The pandemic led to hospital protocols requiring nurses and doctors to wear facial masks for the duration of their shifts. Many of them experienced skin rashes, cheek swellings, acne breakouts, and facial scars where the mask covered their faces. My wife, who is a nurse, was no different. Late one evening, my wife was extremely upset about the acne on her face caused by the long hours wearing the mask. I noticed something odd about the acne. The areas of her face had different shades of redness from the surrounding areas where the acne was most prominent. I had heard rumors about a man-made Morgellons disease which involved micro fibers hiding inside basic surgical hospital masks. So, I quickly ordered two different digital microscopes and one handheld laserscope. What we found on my wife's face was shocking. We discovered those exact same micro-fibers that looked like Morgellons disease in her skin that I had heard about. They appeared as microscopic worm-like cloth fibers projecting from or burrowing in the epidermis. My wife and I took needle-nosed tweezers and were able to extract from her face several of these black micro fibers. We were also able to find several inside of the masks she wore from previous shifts when we placed them under the microscopes. We were able to zoom up close enough that you could see perfect cubed heads at the end of each of the worms and tiny J hooks along the sides of the body. They were very mechanical looking. We compared the man-made Morgellons to several different types of material like hair, clothing threads, rope strands, shaved plastic, and frayed wire, but nothing matched.

My wife asked me, "Why a mask? Why would anyone put these things in a mask?" It was that question that made me realize that everyone is breathing in these microfibers if they are wearing surgical masks. Statistically, the surgical mask was the number one mask required to be worn within medical facilities across our nation. This would unobtrusively provide the opportunity to introduce these microfibers into a vast number of the population. It also dawned on me that the heat and moisture from our breath might be a reason that these fibers become activated. I decided to use a small toothpick to place a tiny water droplet next to the micro fiber and see what would happen. Within just a few seconds, the worm became active. The black microfiber slowly wormed its way closer to the water droplet. I can't say it was alive because they reacted like two mechanisms designed to gravitate towards each other in order for it to function properly. Alone it was harmless, but combined with a missing or complimentary component there would be a reaction.

I later discovered that these fibers were indeed GO. This discovery came to me by way of another researcher who encountered their own similar situation and tested the makeup of the black microfibers in an independent lab. In addition to my discovery, I came across an episode from The Stew Peter's Show. Dr. Carrie Madej, an osteopathic physician, who was a guest on the show and had lab reviewed the Moderna vaccine contents under a microscope in late 2021. Dr. Madej said she had examined the magnified contents of the Moderna, Pfizer, and Johnson & Johnson shots and found it, "very upsetting" to see things in each jab that the manufacturers had not been forthright about. She was so upset that she cried after she verified with a second batch of shots what she had seen in the first vial.

She explained on The Stew Peter's Show that she was first asked by a local Georgian lab to examine under a microscope the contents of a *fresh* Moderna vial which she verified was unaltered before being placed onto a glass slide under a compound microscope. "Nothing was added to the solution, nothing was diluted," she said. "First it looked just translucent. And then as time went on, over two hours, colors appeared. I had never seen anything like this. There wasn't a chemical reaction happening. It was a brilliant blue and royal purple, yellow and sometimes green," she said.

Dr. Madej asked *nanotech engineers* what the emerging brilliant colors might come from. The engineers said, "the only thing they knew that could do that...was a white light, over time, causing a reaction on a super-conducting material." Dr. Madej observed that white light came from the microscope she was using. She noted that an example of a super-conducting substance would be "an injectable computing system." Her comment sounded eerily similar to what the C.E.O of Moderna said regarding their mRNA vaccine being similar to a "*computer operating system.*"

Furthermore, Dr. Madej noticed in the J&J vial that there was

"definitely a substance that looked like **graphene.**

152

They all had **graphene-like structures** in there.
Whether or not they were, I don't have the
capability of testing them in order to know at this
lab, but that's what they appeared to be."
(Emphasis mine).

Sadly, Dr. Madej has been dismissed, demonized, and
character assassinated by mainstream media, most major health
organizations, and various doctors who vehemently stood
against her claims. The reason I give credence to Dr. Madej's
findings is due to finding the GO substance in my wife's
surgical masks and on her face. Clearly the Tech Giants' work
are at hand. Because GO is known to be used within electronics
and optics, it is now conceivable that various types of wireless
direct messaging can be transmitted and now received through
a biosensor device to the human brain.

On February 9, 2022, a Newstarget online article was posted. It
was written by Ramon Tomey who wrote about what the Israeli
intellectual Yuval Noah Harari, a member of the World
Economic Forum (WEF), said,

"Today, we have the technology to **hack human**
beings on a massive scale. Everything is being
digitalized [and] monitored." He goes on to say,
"If you know enough biology and you have
enough computing power and data – you can
hack my **body**, my **brain**, and my life. You can
understand me better than I understand myself.
You can know my personality type, my political
views, and my deepest fears and hopes. And you
can do that not just to me, but to **everyone**."
(Emphasis mine).

The Israeli scholar branded COVID-19 vaccines as tools to usher **surveillance under the skin,**

> "The vaccine will help us, of course. It will make things more manageable, [such as] **surveillance.** People could look back in a hundred years and identify the [COVID-19] pandemic as the moment when a regime of surveillance took over – **especially surveillance under the skin.**" (Emphasis mine).

The idea that the Antichrist will appear to be god-like and later claiming to be god makes more sense now that humans are hackable and more controllable not by the power of suggestion or subliminal messaging, but through bio-technology. The Bible is clear that no matter what torment comes to the people who accept the *mark of the beast*, they will be under a level of physical and mental control never witnessed before in all of human history. Revelation Chp.9 v.6 (ESV) warns us that,

> "…in those days people will **seek death** and **will not find it.** They will long to die, but **death will flee** from them." (Emphasis mine).

I hypothesize that the purpose behind the Covid-19 pandemic was to implement a level of fear that would cunningly coerce people into waving their physical sovereignty and engage in an informal contract with the pharmaceutical industry by allowing the injection of the bio-weapon gene-therapy labeled as a vaccine under *legal fraudulent concealment*. This allowed governments to freely acquire a multitude of human subjects to test how a human *intra-net* would function with digital wireless

154

communication. The only way a human *intra-net* could function properly is through a bio-technology component like graphene oxide. How else could Lucifer and the *sons of disobedience* prevent everyone from buying or selling? I would argue, through surveillance under the skin! Now the *mark of the beast* becomes a feasible reality.

CHAPTER 17

THE FOUR HORSEMEN RIDE: THE RED HORSE

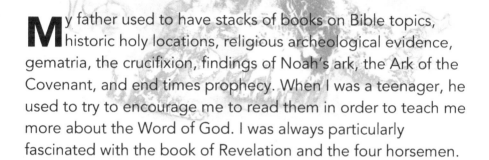

My father used to have stacks of books on Bible topics, historic holy locations, religious archeological evidence, gematria, the crucifixion, findings of Noah's ark, the Ark of the Covenant, and end times prophecy. When I was a teenager, he used to try to encourage me to read them in order to teach me more about the Word of God. I was always particularly fascinated with the book of Revelation and the four horsemen. The red horse of the apocalypse appeared to be the easiest for me to understand. I now recognize that the red horse is far more complex than I first realized. Revelation Chp.6 v.4 (KJV) describes this horse and its rider. It reads,

> "And there went out another horse that was **red**: and **power was given** to him that sat thereon to **take peace** from the earth, and that they should kill one another: and there was given unto him a **great sword**." (Emphasis mine).

Revelation was originally written in Greek. The word red in this verse comes from the Greek word *pyros*. It is translated to mean *fire* or the *color of fire*. John, the author of Revelation, also uses the Greek word *purros* in Revelation Chp.12 v.3 to describe the redness of the Dragon which is in reference to

Satan. *Purros* is translated to mean *ferocious heat* or *wild-like flames.* We can conclude that this horse is not just red, it is riding like a blazing inferno. The New King James Version properly interprets the color of this horse in Revelation Chp.6 v.4 which says,

> "Another horse, **fiery red**, went out. And it was granted to the one who sat on it to take peace from the earth, and that people should kill one another; and there was given to him a great sword." (Emphasis mine).

Most biblical scholars attribute this horse to be entirely about war. I would agree to an extent, but we need to refine what that war looks like in how peace will be taken and how the killings occur.

The ideologies of communist regimes are the antithesis of freedom and have always been represented by the color red. We see this color red on the flags of communist countries. Red has also been associated with left-wing movements in Europe long before the Russian Revolution. The vast majority of communists would characterize themselves as revolutionaries. Most people perceive a revolutionary to be a person of peaceful action trying to bring positive change; however, a revolution always involves suffering, sacrifice, and war which results in the shedding of innocent blood. It is far from peaceful. Loyalists to these dogmas need to eliminate one very crucial element from everyone's life in order for sovereignty to be completely eradicated. That singular component is God.

We are currently a nation heavily bombarded and over powered by Marxist, Socialist, and Communistic regimes that are purposely undermining the unalienable rights endowed by the Creator. Sovereign nations with similar constitutions to the United States thrive on His law being the Supreme Law of the Land. The land is indicative of God's Law when we talk about the Supreme Law of the Land. When referencing His law, you are referencing God's authority over the Earth. Communists deny God and steal the land to be owned by the powerful Elite secretly operating within government institutions. In so doing, God and His law are removed and the People are prevented from owning any of it. Karl Marx summed up the theory of communism when he wrote about the "abolition of private property." Property being that of land. Communist regimes do not want people to own land because the ownership of land gives people a sense of true freedom and independence that the government can't control.

We see this destruction of land in the United States today as nearly 30,000 wildfires had burned approximately 2.5 million acres across the country in 2022 alone. This exceeded the acreage destroyed by fire in over a decade according to the statistics released by the National Interagency Fire Center. In July of 2023, the United Nations (U.N.) Secretary General Antonio Guterres made a statement while speaking at U.N. Headquarters that underscored the need for global action on emissions, climate adaptation, and climate finance. He warned that,

> "The era of global warming has ended" and "the era of **global boiling** has arrived. The air is unbreathable…the heat is unbearable, and the level of fossil fuel profits and climate inaction is unacceptable. Leaders must lead…We can still stop the worst…But to do so we must turn a year

of burning heat into a year of **burning** ambition." (Emphasis mine).

In August 2023, the Maui wildfires that hit Lahaina had curious reports regarding how the fires started. Reports were made by the Hawaiian's that the roads had been blocked off by law enforcement which prevented the people from escaping the blazes. They also stated that government officials had failed to sound the alarm in time for people to evacuate to safety. It is difficult to dismiss the numerous conspiracy theories stating that the Lahaina wildfires in Maui were caused by high-altitude energy beams coming from military drones or satellites because as a U.S. Naval Veteran, I can attest to the fact that we do indeed have such weaponry. The ones I personally witnessed were bolted to the bow of a naval cruiser. Of course, the mainstream media had engaged in their typical damage control through propaganda that twisted the facts and mocked any and all conspiracy theorists contradicting their narrative. These strange beams are reminiscent of fire coming down from the sky. This reminded me of a Bible verse in Revelation I once thought unusual. In light of this potential cause for how the fires began, this verse now makes more sense. Revelation Chp.13 v.11-13 (NKJV) states,

> "Then I saw another beast coming up out of the earth, and he had two horns like a lamb and spoke like a dragon. And he exercises all the authority of the first beast in his presence, and causes the earth and those who dwell in it to worship the first beast, whose deadly wound was healed. He performs great signs, so that **he** even **makes fire come down** from heaven on the earth **in the sight of men.**" (Emphasis mine).

160

On September 13, 2023, Julia Jacob and Dan Peck wrote an article for ABC News that stated,

> "Record-breaking wildfires have occurred all over the northern hemisphere during 2023. The total wildfires emissions for 2023 has been estimated to be almost 410 megatons."

It is becoming more obvious that the rider of the red horse of the apocalypse is given two powerful weapons. Fire is its first weapon and used to suffocate free thinking and a prosperous people who own land and buildings that host their pursuit of happiness once protected by His law. As a former gubernatorial candidate in one of the largest nation states of America, I became privy to information the average person would never know about. When I was campaigning during the California Recall against Gavin Newsom and in the 2022 gubernatorial election cycle, I spoke with countless people whose homes and businesses were unfortunately burned down during California's wildfires between 2017 and 2020. Many had insurance and their insurance claims were approved for their property. However, these afflicted Californians were told by representatives of their county, city, and from the banks that they could not rebuild on the land their home or business had been built on and they would need to take their money and purchase property elsewhere. Others were told by county Utility and District Supervisors that water mains and electricity were going to be shut down for an unforeseeable amount of time for the seared land that was now deemed a hazardous zone and was requiring further investigation and assessment of damages before they could be reinstated. At first, the information given out by local government appeared reasonable and legitimate. It wasn't until several families reached out to my campaign enraged that their land or commercial property in these zones had been bought out from underneath them that this became questionably unjust. Of course, I was disheartened to learn that the California state and U.S. federal government agencies were the culprits behind illegally selling millions of acres of declared hazardous wastelands they had no rights to. They had sold the lands to front companies who appeared to be American based, but were indeed owned by foreign government organizations and their aristocrats. These front companies varied from science laboratories to real estate associations from agriculture mega corps to affluent private partnerships, but don't take my word for it. I encourage you to do your own due diligence to find the same information I dug up. The families and individuals who endured the aftermath of those devastating fires swelled with fury and indignation that could be seen behind their eyes. Who could blame them? They lost everything. Years of thriving independent businesses burned to the ground with no ability to start new. Land past down from two or three generations now gone up in smoke and stolen from them with no apparent justice in sight. Homes built from the ground up now smolder without a chance to rebuild and start anew.

This is the power of the red horse in taking peace from the Earth. It will be physical fire that will exasperate even the most patient of people into violence. Many Californians today proclaim that they would simply leave their state or country and seek better horizons with more open scenery to buy new property in order to remain unscathed by the corruption before they entertain the idea of participating in any defense to preserve their sovereignty. It is irrelevant if these fires truly are a false flag operation induced by sympathizers operating within the walls of federal and state agencies to orchestrate the ability to buy up the property for personal profit or for foreign benefit. It is the chaos from the fiery madness that will ensnare the meek who will become volatile upon their neighbor. Deviants who hide in the shadows and think nobody sees them and nobody knows who they are, will eventually utilize false flag tactics to induce their next great world war. Here is something to consider, you can either fight here today or somewhere else tomorrow. Involving yourself now within your local government is one of the best first steps in fighting back peacefully. Those seeking refuge elsewhere will soon find that there will be nowhere else to go if they continue to hide from their responsibility as a contributing member of their community for sound governance. You are either going to standup for our natural God-given rights or decide to go quietly into the night! You will either be hot or cold, left or right, good or evil, there will be no lukewarm middle ground.

The second weapon the rider of the red horse is given is a *great sword*. It is not described in what way the *great sword* will be used by the rider, so we must look to scripture to find potential explanations on how the sword will be used. The Greek word *romfaia* describes a sword used as a weapon of war, but the *great sword* of the horseman is translated from the Greek word *machaira megalee*. Through my research, I discovered that *machaira* is a knife used to prepare a sacrifice or to slaughter animals for food. *Machaira* is also a sword worn by executioners and judges. The red horseman's sword is described as *great* which is translated from the word *megalee*. This means the knife is either very large or is longer than usual and is extremely precise in performing its purpose. Leviticus Chp.26 v.25 (NKJV) says,

"I will bring a **sword** against you that will execute

the **vengeance** of My covenant." (Emphasis mine).

Jeremiah Chp.12 v.12 (ESV) further states that,

> "Upon all the bare heights in the desert-
> destroyers have come, for the **sword** of
> the LORD **devours** from one end of **the land** to the
> other; **no flesh has peace.**" (Emphasis mine).

These verses perfectly illustrate that God uses His sword to execute His vengeance to devour the land upon all who have forgotten their covenant with Him. His law is enacted upon the land through the judgment of His sword.

The *great sword* will be used to swipe away what remains of His law written in the hearts of men and therefore His peace will also be removed. Philippians Chp.4 v.7 (ESV) says,

> "The **peace of God**, which surpasses all
> understanding, will **guard** your **hearts** and your
> **minds** in Christ Jesus." (Emphasis mine).

The *peace of God* which transcends all understanding means that the *peace* associated with God cannot just simply be explained by human intelligence. It is spiritually experienced and felt in a way that words cannot adequately express. Jeremiah said that "no flesh has peace." It is frightening to know that human beings are not the only ones who will experience the loss of peace. This expulsion of peace will be felt by all animals, all fish in the sea, birds of the air, and creatures along the ground. God's guardianship and protection over the hearts and minds of all those who have ignored His law in exchange for lascivious and unethical statutes will be withdrawn.

Hebrews Chp.13 v.20 (ESV) describes God as,

> "…the **God of peace** who brought again from the
> dead our Lord Jesus, the great shepherd of the
> sheep, by the blood of the eternal covenant."
> (Emphasis mine).

The Bible is distinctively saying to know God, Jesus, is to know peace. In order to successfully remove peace that we now know means to know God, God and His law must be removed from all lands.

The area of enterprise that the fiery red horse will consume during his gallop is constitutional law. Remember, power is *given* to the rider of the red horse to take peace from the Earth. Fire will literally consume the lands by way of false flags that will lead to civil and revolutionary war and a greater world war. Sovereign lands and people will later be controlled by a one world government regime utilizing both communistic and Fabien tactics. Communism will use brute force and the Fabien strategy will accomplish their goals through permeation in targeting liberal politicians and extreme social activists influencing public policy by way of gradualism. They will be like a viper slowly squeezing its game before poisoning and devouring its prey.

At the writing of this book, America is now entering into the 2024 Presidential race and many believers are putting their hopes into Trump. They are praying he will be the saving grace to the United States and bring peace once more to the land of the free, home of the brave. They have forgotten to put their prayers and focus on God healing our land and restoring His law in our country. Instead, they pray that Trump will be put into office in order to be that source of restoration. The Bible tells us to pray for those in authority in 1 Timothy Chp.2 v.1-2 (NIV) which says,

> "I urge, then, first of all, that petitions, **prayers**, intercession and thanksgiving be made for all people—for kings and **all those in authority**, that we may live **peaceful** and quiet lives in all godliness and holiness." (Emphasis mine).

It is not wrong to pray for the representatives of our country or to pray for a servant of the People to be put into power, but I caution you not to forget that it is God working through that servant that brings restoration. All glory must first and foremost go to God.

Now consider one more possible way peace could be removed from America. President Donald J. Trump may possibly become president once more. I have spoken to many registered democrats who do not plan to vote for Joe Biden in the next presidential election. If that is the case and President Trump regains his seat, it is conceivable that an assassination attempt could be planned by the *sons of disobedience*. A plan may already be in motion. It would stand to reason that America is primed for a civil and revolutionary war if President Trump is killed because his popularity has united a significant majority of the country. To make matters worse, it is also possible that the electric grid may come down or a major attack on one of America's largest cities or at least an important unsuspecting area of the country will likely occur in conjunction with the timing of President Trump's second term…I hope I am wrong!

Members like that of the W.E.F. will, no doubt, work tirelessly to make sure President Trump does not stand in their way of progress. The *Great Sword* in my opinion is the *Great Reset*. As Klaus Schwab, W.E.F. Chairman said,

"You will own nothing and be happy."

Klaus's idea of owning nothing is a brutal sacrifice, a slaughter he and his W.E.F. cronies expect the rest of the world to accept while they horde power of ownership and privacy for themselves. On August 24, 2021, Resilience posted an online article written by Ivan Wecke in their economy section that was originally published by the digital media platform, Open Democracy. It beautifully summarized *The Great Reset*. Ivan said,

> "The set of conspiracy theories around the Great Reset are nebulous and hard to pin down, but piecing them together gives us something like this: the Great Reset is the global elite's plan to instate a **communist** world order by **abolishing private property** while using COVID-19 to solve overpopulation and enslaving what remains of humanity with vaccines… At the heart of conspiracy theories are supposed secret agendas and malicious intent. While these may be absent from the WEF's Great Reset initiative, what I found was something almost as sinister hiding in plain sight. In fact, more sinister because it's real and it's happening now. And it involves things as fundamental as our food, our data and our

vaccines…'**Stakeholder capitalism**'…The idea is that global capitalism should be transformed so that corporations no longer focus solely on serving shareholders but become custodians of society by creating value for customers, suppliers, employees, communities and other stakeholders. The way the WEF sees stakeholder capitalism being carried out is through a range of multi-stakeholder partnerships bringing together the private sector, governments and civil society across all areas of world governance. The idea of stakeholder capitalism and multi-stakeholder partnerships might sound warm and fuzzy, until we dig deeper and realize that **this actually means giving corporations more power over society, and democratic institutions less.**" (Emphasis mine).

The *sons of disobedience* require your fealty. Their statutes, mandates, regulations, and ordinances must have the power to supersede His law. Christ believers to a great extent have forgotten the Law of God. Many churches and church followers have supported and performed same sex marriages. This goes completely against God's Law that warns against such abominations as we read in Romans Chp.1 v.26-27 (ESV) that says,

"For this reason, God gave them up to dishonorable passions. For their **women exchanged natural relations for those that are contrary to nature;** and the **men likewise gave up natural relations with women** and were consumed with passion for one another, **men committing shameless acts with men** and **receiving in**

themselves the due penalty for their error."
(Emphasis mine).

It is now undeniable why His sword will sweep across all lands removing what little remains of His law and allowing a great sacrificial slaughter to take place under barbaric and tyrannical regimes. Psalms Chp.28 v.5 (NASB) tells us that

> "Because **they do not regard** the works of **the Lord**
> Nor the **deeds of His hands,**
> **He will tear them down** and **not build them up.**"
> (Emphasis mine).

The fiery red horse of the apocalypse will be granted the power to burn it all to the ground because the People and the Will of the People can no longer be sheltered by the *Laws of Nature and of Nature's God* when they disregard His law.

CHAPTER 18

THE FOUR HORSEMEN RIDE: THE BLACK HORSE

I have often wondered if the people I walk past, drive by, or acquainted myself with truly understand the depth of how absolutism has grossly impoverished the very essence of what it means to live in prosperity. Many people spend the majority of their life working long hours in their occupations hoping to one day delight in the fruits of their labor with a retirement that is a rightful reward. However grand or minuscule, pensions have been the bright light at the end of many laborious careers. Retirement requires a level of earned, invested, or bartered wealth in order to sustain any form of living subsidy. Unfortunately, that sustainment will come to an end because gold and silver will eventually no longer hold its worth as we read in Ezekiel Chp.7 v.19 (NIV) which says,

> "They will throw their **silver** into the streets, and their **gold** will be treated as **a thing unclean**. Their silver and gold **will not** be able to **deliver them** in the day of the **LORD's wrath**. It will not satisfy their hunger or fill their stomachs, for it has caused them to stumble into sin." (Emphasis mine).

America and every other nation are quickly entering into a time of famine. Not just the kind of famine we typically think of as defined in the Merriam Webster dictionary as "an extreme scarcity of food," but a famine of moral character, unhindered honesty, and the presence of just-men. Those who built America dug their hands into the ground and tilled the land for harvest, put their backs into building their own homes with the desire to lay down roots, hunted for their food, educated their children, and defended life with zeal. An individual who stood with principal was respected and distinguished in that time. Such magnanimous people, in my humble opinion, scarcely remain. I will admit no generation is or was perfect, but it is this last generation mentioned in Revelation that will endure the judgement of their virtuous acts compared with their wrongful deeds. It is because of such moral decay that the rider of the black horse will be released upon all mankind. Revelation Chp.6 v.5-6 (NKJV) describes the unveiling of the black horse,

> "When He opened the third seal, I heard the third living creature say, 'Come and see.' So, I looked, and behold, a **black horse**, and he who sat on it had a **pair of scales** in his hand. And I heard a voice in the midst of the four living creatures saying, 'A **quart of wheat** for a **denarius**, and **three quarts of barley** for a **denarius**; and do not harm the **oil** and the **wine**.'" (Emphasis mine).

There is a multitude of cataclysm with the events of the black horse. The rider reveals the devastating consequences of economic instability. Commerce and world finance will destructively implode. Corruption, debt, inflation, stock market boom and busts, unemployment, financial loss, and a failure of truth and justice prevailing will be unlike anything the world has ever undergone before. Poverty will be at an all-time high, food shortages and careful rationing during times of intense scarcity will set in. Travel and drink will be protected in some mannerism, but only for those who can afford it. We need to be paying attention to the actions and inactions of the unscrupulous in government when it comes to the time of this rider so that the innocent and the dormant can be forewarned in hopes that they can safeguard against this horseman's onslaught.

The black horseman's weapon are scales. We must keep in mind when looking at the original context and language that there can be more than one meaning behind God's word and all of them must be taken into account. The word *scales* in Greek is *axios* which means *worthy*. According to Strong's Concordance, *axios* can also translate to "of weight, of worth, deserving, comparable or suitable." Interesting to note, this rider is not just holding scales, but a *pair of scales*. The term *pair of scales* is derived from the Greek *zugon* which means *yoke*. Many biblical scholars will compare this to the yoke of an oxen used to ease the work of hauling or pulling heavy loads. In this case, the yoke symbolizes servitude or carrying the burden of a task or mission. 2 Corinthians Chp.6 v.14-16 (NKJV) warns,

> "Do not be **unequally yoked** together with unbelievers. For what **fellowship** has righteousness with lawlessness? And what **communion** has light with darkness? And what **accord** has Christ with Belial? Or what **part** has a believer with an unbeliever? And what **agreement** has the temple of God with idols?" (Emphasis mine).

There can be no pact with amoral politicians and government councils. They take advantage of fair minded and balanced

173

communities to increase their dominance. They overburden an honest people into despotism. This can be seen in how America is experiencing a level of taxation without representation unlike anything this nation has been subjected to in its history. The weight on the People's shoulders have been exacerbated by the unbalanced pull of uncouthly servants in places of governmental authority creating an unequally yoked burden upon a fair-minded populace.

The wielding of the scales is also a representation of unyoked commerce amongst the world's economic system forced upon the innocent by unprincipled powers who will all be measured in kind and found wanting. This harbinger will bring turmoil as seen in the words of the living creature who says, "a quart of wheat for a denarius, and three quarts of barley for a denarius." This is an indication of economic disparity and a sign that obtaining food will be heavily impacted. The Greek word *denarius* means a *day's wage*. This verse states that a quart of wheat and three quarts of barley will cost the equivalent of a day's wage. In other words, it will take a full day of work just to put basic sustenance on the table for a single meal.

It is strangely prophetic that meat is not mentioned in this verse. Even today, meat is more expensive than any grain. It is interesting to note that livestock, poultry, and cattle are predominantly fed grain. These animals require four or five pounds of grain to produce a single pound of meat. According to this scripture, wheat will be three times as expensive as barley when this seal is broken. This attests to the probability that farming conditions may potentially cause barley to be easier to grow and wheat more laborious. The expense in its production will ultimately lead to a scarcity in the amount of meat available for the purpose of general consumption.

Because meat is the primary course of the everyday meal on menus in most restaurants, small eateries, and local venues, they will more than likely be forced to close. This will contribute to thousands of job losses.

As I've said before, the *sons of disobedience* have to tell you their plans before they do it. How they reveal their hand is evident to those who have eyes to see and ears to hear. There have been rumors of government agriculture agencies, including the USDA, sending letters to farmers financially incentivizing them not to farm or grow crops under the guise of conservation land management. The timing of the letters led to strange rumors about farmers forced to destroy their crops because they were sent during the initiation of the Covid-19 lockdowns. Farmers found themselves with more production than they could sell due to restaurants, diners, and bistros closing up shop or shutting down all together. The Biden administration, is currently encouraging farmers to leave some of their land fallow as part of the Conservation Reserve Program (CRP). The USDA states the purpose of CRP which was signed into law in 1985 by President Ronald Reagan was to re-establish valuable land cover to help improve water quality, prevent soil erosion, and reduce loss of the wildlife habitat. The fact that government is paying famers not to grow crops deceptively hides that this is destroying food production and, therefore, supply through a reduction in crop output in the name of land conservation umbrellaed by climate change. The more government can regulate farming production, the more they can declare who eats and who doesn't based on any fable narrative they desire hidden under the pretense of good farming practices.

Throughout 2022, America was victim to a staggering number

of unusual fires occurring across our nation that involved many food processing facilities. Melanie Risdon reported in a Rangefire.us online article that,

"Food shortages have been exacerbated by a string of fires, plane crashes and explosions at nearly two dozen food processing facilities across...the U.S. The most recent happened...in Georgia when a small plane crashed shortly after takeoff into a General Mills plant just east of Atlanta...A massive fire...destroyed parts of the Azure Standard Headquarters in Oregon, a company that self-describes as 'the USA's largest independent food distributor'...Firefighters contended with a massive blaze at Taylor Farms packaged salad plant in Salinas, Calif. ...An airplane crashed into Idaho's Gem State Processing facility...Firefighters from several departments in Maine helped battle a massive fire that destroyed East Conway Beef & Pork butcher shop and meat market in Center Conway, N.H. ...a major fire...forced the closure of the Nestle plant in Jonesboro, Ark. ...A fire at the Maricopa Food Pantry, a food bank in Arizona, saw 50,000 pounds worth of food burn up and yet another blaze at the Texas-based Rio Fresh severely damaged the onion processing facility. A portion of Wisconsin River Meats was destroyed by fire...Another fire sparked by a boiler explosion at a potato chip plant south of Hermiston, Ore. ...Another fire caused the Louis Dreyfus Company's Claypool, Ind. soybean processing and biodiesel plant...to suspend production...A fire caused more than $100,000 in damages to a San Antonio food processing plant...Fire engulfed the Maid-Rite Steak Co. food processing plant in Lackawanna County, Pennsylvania...Fire consumed JBS USA beef processing plant in Grand Island, Neb. ...Another raging fire severely damaged the Patak Meat Production company in Austell, Ga. ...Firefighters battled a large fire at the River Valley Ingredients plant in Hanceville, Ala."

These are not just flukes or mere coincidences. The multitude of events befalling America's food industries resembles that of a rehearsed controlled demolition.

According to data from the Federal Railroad Administration in 2022, there were more than 1,164 train derailments across the country that year. That means the country is averaging roughly three derailments per day. Of course, not all of these derailments are like the calamitous accident in East Palestine, OH where a Norfolk Southern train carrying hazardous materials derailed near the small town. None the less, they are happening. This is vastly significant because the production and delivery of America's food supply chain is very easily disrupted. It becomes apparent how the rider of the black horse could manifest the predicted burdensome expense along with the scarcity of food. It is important to note that even in the time of the end, those that remain who realize that Jesus is the only way are to recognize His glory and show their devotion. The representation of the cost of the grain is also a representation of the value of Jesus in our lives who is often referred to as the Bread of Life.

Californian taxes are nearly the highest in all of the United States. Merchantry representatives go unchecked when they allow for inflation to become unbearable. Currently California has the highest average in gas prices at $5.80 per gallon in San Bernardino, San Diego, Ventura, and San Francisco. Many people, including myself have posted this on their social media pages and shown gasoline prices as high as $6.59 per gallon. President Donald Trump in early 2023 warned of a $7 per gallon gasoline price if he was not to be re-elected. A cost of $7.39 for a gallon of regular gasoline was posted by a TikTok user at a Mobil gas station in Los Angeles in late 2023.

Fox News Economist, Thomas Catenacci, published an online piece on October 19, 2022, that explains the pervasive bureaucracy of California's ludicrous pump prices in an exceptionally simplistic manner. He said,

> "Economists and oil market experts sharply criticized Gov. Gavin Newsom, D-Calif., for his recent rhetoric blaming 'greedy oil companies' for high gasoline prices in California…They [California Legislators] have a bunch of idiotic policies…You'd have to explain why [oil companies are] ripping people off 50% more in California than the rest of the world and why they only choose to do it now…For example, the state requires refiners to produce a higher-grade gasoline, which is generally costlier for consumers during the summer months to protect air quality. In addition, regulations make it hard for companies to build new refineries, increase refinery capacity or boost oil production in the state…But the source of high gas prices is simple:

government restrictions on supply. Try building a
new refinery in California, to make California
special gas."

As the cost of everything increases at a rate that people are
struggling to keep up with, poverty naturally swells. America
has over a 600 thousand homeless population, a number that
exceeds the state of Wyoming's general registered by census
population. California alone accounts for nearly one-third of
America's homeless population at around 175 thousand and
growing. America's open borders proliferates the homelessness
when people illegally pass through who don't speak the official
national language, who don't know the culture, who don't know
the Supreme Law of the Land, who don't know the state laws
they've trespassed into, and who have entered into a land
where businesses have little demand for their skill sets. It is by
no surprise that poverty and the control of oil, which is not to
be harmed by this horseman, are connected. According to the
Energy Information Administration's (EIA) report,

"Gasoline is the most-consumed petroleum
product in the United States. In 2022,
consumption of finished motor gasoline averaged
about 8.78 million b/d (369 million gallons per
day), which was about 43% of total U.S. petroleum
consumption. Finished motor gasoline includes
fuel ethanol.

Distillate fuel oil is the second-most-consumed
petroleum product in the United States. Distillate
fuel oil includes diesel fuel and heating oil. Diesel
fuel is used in diesel engines which are often in
heavy construction equipment, trucks, buses,
tractors, boats, trains, some automobiles, and

electricity generators. Heating oil, also called fuel oil, is used for heating homes and buildings in boilers and furnaces, for industrial heating, and for producing electricity in power plants. In 2022, total distillate fuel oil consumption averaged about 3.96 million b/d (166 million gallons per day), which was 20% of total U.S. petroleum consumption.

Hydrocarbon gas liquids (HGLs) the third-most-used category of petroleum in the United States, include propane, ethane, butane, and other HGLs that are produced at natural gas processing plants and oil refineries. HGLs have many uses. Total consumption of HGLs in 2022 averaged about 3.59 million b/d, accounting for about 18% of total petroleum consumption.

Jet fuel is the fourth-most-used petroleum product in the United States. Jet fuel consumption averaged about 1.56 million b/d (65 million gallons per day) in 2022, accounting for about 8% of total petroleum consumption."

The rider of the black horse is instructed to "hurt not the oil and the wine." This may be due to the fact that crude oil will be heavily controlled by the Elites and God will take from them what they've used to restrain the meek. Because crude corporatists have increased the cost of basic transportation, they will make travel incredibly difficult as we are already starting to see worldwide before this horse begins its gallop. In addition, there are 15-minute cities rumored to be in design. These cities are in development in order to keep the populace from traveling any further than 10 miles from their homes.

Oil and wine are known to be used for cooking and medicinal purposes as well. We've already seen from the course of the white horse that the medical industry will be heavily inundated by nefarious policies that will limit a doctor's Hippocratic Oath to "abstain from all intentional wrong-doing and harm." People will undoubtedly have to become their own self-proclaimed medical practitioners making tried and true holistic remedies more important than they've been known to be in modern times. God may be preserving the means of their medicinal properties during the release of this harbinger because of the economic upheaval and shortage of medicine that will make them necessary for survival.

Another reason that the oil and wine may be untouched is because they are used as offerings to God. Oil and the wine were key elements of the *sheaf* which is a wave offering on the first day following the 7th Sabbath after Pesach and Unleavened Bread. In addition, the fiftieth day (Pentecost) was memorialized as the type and foreshadowing of Christ's pouring out of the Holy Spirit upon the people and the birth of His Church as we read in Leviticus Chp.23 v.11-13 (NKJV) which establishes the feast of Passover, *Pesach,*

> "He shall wave the sheaf before the LORD, to be accepted on your behalf; on the day after the Sabbath the priest shall wave it. And you shall offer on that day, when you wave the sheaf, a male lamb of the first year, without blemish, as a burnt offering to the LORD. Its **grain** offering shall be two-tenths of an ephah of fine flour mixed with **oil**, an offering made by fire to the LORD, for a sweet aroma; and its **drink offering** shall be of **wine**, one-fourth of a hin." (Emphasis mine).

Oil in both the Old and New Testament is often illustrated that it had sanctifying or cleansing properties. In essence, when someone consecrates and sanctifies something with oil, they set it apart for God's use. Jesus encouraged his followers to anoint themselves with oil whenever they took up the practice of fasting and to pour oil on the sick as part of the healing process. Wine was also shared during the Last Supper, which signified the new covenant with Jesus and will still be required when taking up communion during the end times for new Christ believers.

Furthermore, the oil and the wine altogether speak to the sacrifice that Christ made for our sins. Therefore, it may be a fair assumption that God does not want believers who are baptized during these times and are covered by the blood of Christ to be harmed or be measured by the *pair of scales* of judgment from this rider. A well-known use of *scales* in the sense of passing judgement appears in the book of Daniel. Daniel Chp.5 v.25-28 (ESV) reads,

> "And this is the writing that was inscribed: MENE, MENE, TEKEL, and PARSIN. This is the interpretation of the matter: MENE, God has numbered the days of your kingdom and brought it to an end; TEKEL, you have been **weighed** in **the balances** and **found wanting**; PERES, your kingdom is divided and given to the Medes and Persians." (Emphasis mine).

God tells Belshazzar through Daniel's interpretation, "You have been weighed in the balances, and found wanting." This means that Belshazzar had not lived up to the Lord's expectations. It is certainly possible that God wants everyone to understand His power is complete and His divine judgment on humanity will be caused by their greed and violent oppression upon those who are to inherit the Earth.

Lastly, the color black must not be overlooked. It is often associated with mourning and destruction in the Bible. In the context of the black horse, it visually represents the distress that follows scarcity which leads to famine. It is by no stretch of the imagination that the area of enterprise the black horse takes hold of is the oil industry and matches the color of trade. It is also the color of the robe judges wear in many nations and symbolizes how justice is blind. Judgement will no doubt harshly come upon the judicial system and officers of the courts who have allowed for criminals to be victimized and victims to be criminalized. Isaiah Chp.5 v.22-23 (NIV) warns,

> "Woe to those...who **acquit the guilty** for a bribe but **deny justice to the innocent.**" (Emphasis mine).

Romans Chp.2 v.3 (CSB) further cautions,

> "**Do you think**—anyone of you who judges those who do such things yet do the same—that **you will escape God's judgment?**" (Emphasis mine).

CHAPTER 19

THE FOUR HORSEMEN RIDE: THE PALE HORSE

The four horsemen of Revelation will bring calamity unlike any other time in history. The pervasive unrest will draw people to desire to take their own life in an effort to escape the cataclysms. Death comes for all of us. I pity those that feel the need to end the gift of life they believe is no longer worth living irrelevant of the grueling trials they may have been dealt. Those trials are what teach us and shape us into stronger, resilient, and more prosperous human beings. Just as gold is refined by fire, it is God's design to refine the human spirit by fiery trials. The taking of one's own life is still considered murder, regardless of the rationale behind the action, according to the Bible which makes it clear that our lives are not ours to take as we read in 1 Corinthians Chp.6 v.19-20 (NIV),

> "Do you not know that your **bodies are temples** of the Holy Spirit, who is in you, whom you have received from God? **You are not your own; you were bought at a price**. Therefore, honor God with your bodies." (Emphasis mine).

Exodus Chp.20 v.13 (NIV) also states that

> "**You shall not murder.**" (Emphasis mine).

185

Canada is currently advertising, while practically glorifying, the law they passed in June of 2016 that was recently amended in 2023 and titled Medical Assistance in Dying (MAID). This program legally allows euthanasia for the terminally ill, disabled, or chronically diseased adults. The subtle underlying purpose behind the promotion of this program is population control. They mask this intent through emphasizing the need to minimize an overburdening population. The Canadians consider them to be useless and no longer capable of contributing productively to society. Rather than valuing every remaining minute of life one is given, the Canadian government bolsters mercy killings under the guise of helping those end their life who in their opinion lack a quality of life.

According to the 2022 World Deaths Statistics, roughly 7 million people died that year out of a current worldwide population of around 8 billion. This is nearly 9% of the human race that died under various circumstances in a single year. When the last horseman is set free, a horrific death toll that will dwarf 7 million will cast its horrifying shadow upon humanity as Revelation Chp.6 v.8 (KJV) says,

> "And I looked, and behold **a pale horse**: and **his name** that sat on him was **Death**, and **Hell** followed with him. And power was given unto **them** over **the fourth part** of the **earth**, to **kill** with sword, and with hunger, and with death, and with the beasts of the earth." (Emphasis mine).

The horse is described as *pale*. The word *pale* is translated from the Greek word *chloros*. It is from this Greek root word that we get the English word *Chlorophyll* and *Chlorine* which means *green*. Revelation uses the word *chloros* in other verses as well.

We see it used in Revelation Chp.8 v.7 (KJV) that says,

> "The first angel sounded, and there followed hail and fire mingled with blood, and they were cast upon the earth: and the third part of trees was burnt up, and all **green** (*chloros*) grass was burnt up." (Emphasis mine).

It is used again in Revelation Chp.9 v.4 (KJV) which states,

> "And it was commanded them that they should not hurt the grass of the earth, neither any **green** (*chloros*) thing, neither any tree; but only those men which have not the seal of God **in** their foreheads." (Emphasis mine).

Now it becomes apparent that this horse is not a pale white or ash colored horse, but a pale green horse. It is like the putrid green hue of people's skin when they are sick which is typically associated with nausea and resulting in that decaying feeling. This is probably a more accurate description of the color labeled for this rider.

This rider is also the only one who is given a name which is *Death*. Because of this, we can reason that human demise must be tied to the color of the horse. If a dead body is left unattended, the body typically bloats from gasses produced from internal decomposition. The decomposition generally makes the body increase in size and turn a greenish color followed by putrification. Blood and foam will begin to seep from the mouth which always attracts insects often increasing high levels of bacteria and adding to this change in skin tone.

The description of what this rider brings is truly dreadful. But notice, there is not just one rider with the pale green horse. There are two riders according to Revelation Chp.6 v.8 (KJV) which says,

> "...and his name that sat on him was **Death**, and **Hell followed** with him. And power was given unto **them**." (Emphasis mine).

Hell that follows is indicating more than just an underworld. It is a *prosopopaeia* or a personification. The verse declares, "power was given unto them." The word *them* is a plural pronoun. In other translations, it is not the place of Hell that follows but rather *Hades*. *Sheol* (Hades) is spoken of as a state, condition, or a place where the dead are received according to the Hebrew language of the Old Testament. The name *Hades* (Haides) is translated from Greek to mean *unseen* or *the unseen one*. In this instance, it would not be much of a stretch to interpret the words to mean *the unseen horse and its rider was Hades*. The Christian Standard Bible renders a more accurate interpretation to Revelation Chp.6 v.8 when it says,

> "And I looked, and there was a **pale green horse**. Its rider was named Death, **Hades** was following after him." (Emphasis mine).

According to Greek mythology Hades is depicted as a cold ruthless ruler who brings you into hellish torment. This is contrary to Hollywood's depiction of Hades whose purpose was not to judge but to ensure that the souls who entered his domain were treated according to their deeds in life. He acts as a warden who can be negotiated with. However, this now makes more sense why the word *them* is used and a sense of personification is implied to the riders.

The amount of extermination Death and Hades will bring is harrowingly on the horizon. They are given power over one-fourth of the earth to kill. If there are roughly 8 billion people on the Earth, one-fourth of 8 billion is 2 billion people who will end up meeting a painful and untimely departure from this Earth. The second half of Revelation Chp.6 v.8 (KJV) reveals how this will occur,

> "…And power was given unto **them** over the fourth part of the earth, to **kill** with **sword**, and with **hunger**, and with **death**, and with the **beasts of the earth**." (Emphasis mine).

2 billion people will be killed by sword, hunger, death, and with beasts of the Earth. The word *sword* in this verse is not the same as the meaning of the word used with the fiery red horse. The Greek word *rhomphaia* in this verse is the source of the translation for *sword*. This is a large, slightly curved, and single edged sword designed to thrust and slash the enemy. It was used as a weapon in battle between 300-500 B.C. predominantly for the purpose of war during close combat encounters. This is a clear identifier that one-fourth of those 2 billion people will be killed in a close combat war.

At the writing of this book, America is not only involved in the Ukraine Russian conflict, but is also muddled into the Israeli and Palestinian fracas by providing 6 billion dollars to Iran for a prisoner exchange deal and 14.5 billion dollars to Israel in military aid. This clash appears to be dragging the rest of the world into a potential third world war to which the death toll of 500 million worldwide is now looking extremely possible. To

LUCIFER ZENITH / DANIEL R. MERCURI

give you a rough visual of that number, the current United States census indicates that there are potentially 300-330 million people living in America. The death of one-third of 2 billion people would result in the wipe out of the entire American nation.

Another group of people will be killed with hunger. In Greek, this word translates from *peina* which means *starvation*. Wars and skirmishes always seem to bring destruction to various infrastructures such as communication and electrical modes, supply chains, water lines, gas conduits, emergency medical dispatches, and travel. It would stand to reason that even the most basic of needs will not be accessible during these riders' conquests. Other Old Testament scriptures paint haunting pictures of what this type of hunger will look like. Isaiah Chp.29 v.8 (NASB1995) says,

> "It will be as when a hungry man dreams,
> And behold, he is eating;
> But **when he awakens,** his **hunger is not satisfied,**
> Or as when a thirsty man dreams,
> And behold, he is drinking, but **when he awakens,**
> behold, **he is faint,** and his thirst is not quenched.
> Thus, the multitude of **all the nations will be**
> Who wage war against Mount Zion." (Emphasis mine).

Lamentations Chp.4 v.9 (NASB1995) also says,

> "**Better** are those **slain with the sword,** Than those **slain with hunger;** For they pine away, being stricken. For lack of the fruits of the field."
> (Emphasis mine).

The kind of hunger that will befall another 500 million will for certain be caused from wars fought on all fronts in every nation. No one will be able to escape it which will be by design in order for there to be a one world system to bring *order out of chaos* that all mankind will beg for.

The next source of human demise will be from death. I have often wondered, how one could kill with death? I never really understood the meaning behind this portion of the verse. When I had asked various pastors or Christians throughout my years about their viewpoint of its meaning, no one really had an answer. My spirit always felt as though the explanations fell short of the complete intention of its use because they were always vague and filled with generalities or given with the statement that it meant people were going to die in great multitude. It has taken me years to gain a wiser level of perspective. Let me clarify. The act of killing *brings* death which is not up for debate, but Revelation Chp.6 v.8 says to kill *with* death. In that case, death appears to be a weapon.

According to the W.H.O.,

> "Human remains only pose a substantial risk to health in a few special cases, such as deaths from cholera or hemorrhagic fevers.
>
> Workers who routinely handle corpses may however risk contracting tuberculosis, bloodborne viruses (e.g. hepatitis B and C and HIV) and gastrointestinal infections (e.g. cholera, E. coli, hepatitis A, rotavirus diarrhea, salmonellosis, shigellosis and typhoid/paratyphoid fevers):

- Tuberculosis can be acquired if the bacillus is aerosolized – residual air in lungs exhaled, fluid from lungs spurted up through the nose or mouth during handling of the corpse.
- Bloodborne viruses can be transmitted via direct contact of non-intact skin or mucous membrane from splashing of blood or body fluid or from injury from bone fragments and needles.
- Gastrointestinal (GI) infections can easily be transmitted from feces leaked from dead bodies. Transmission occurs via the fecal–oral route through direct contact with the body, soiled clothes or contaminated vehicles or equipment. GI infections can also be spread as a result **of contamination of the water supply with dead bodies.**" (Emphasis mine).

As of December 18, 2023, California and the City of Los Angeles are planning on recycling sewage and waste water into drinking water. This brings to light how a "contamination of the water supply with dead bodies" could occur. Colorado and California are the only two states who are currently engaged in this dangerous proposal. It is the dying and the dead bodies that will bring pestilence. This would confirm other biblical translations of this chapter and verse. The English Standard Version of Revelation Chp.6 v.8 reads,

"…and they were given authority over a fourth of the earth, to kill with sword and with famine and

with pestilence and by wild beasts of the earth." (Emphasis mine).

Undoubtedly, there will be killings by various types of diseases that could be brought on by biological weapons from external or internal sources. Many people today believe that the Covid-19 gene therapy injection, which is masquerading as a vaccine, is indeed a biological weapon. Its nefarious effects may not be felt around the world until a few more years have passed. This will potentially align with the rider of the pale green horse and the unseen horseman.

Pestilence is also in reference to pests such as bugs, insects, and other creepy crawling creatures. In California, the Aedes aegypti mosquitoes are on the rise. They are one of more than 3,500 mosquito species and are a dangerous invasive insect that has spread diseases like Dengue, Zika, Chikungunya, and yellow fever in other countries. Pests not only infect humans, but they also have a tendency to destroy various crops and disrupt the food supply. A USA Today online article written on April 30, 2023, by Janet Loehrke depicts an example of how pests can affect our food resources. She wrote,

> "In areas of the Northeast where the colorful but invasive spotted lanternfly is emerging, killing season has arrived. The next generation of crop-destroying pest has hatched in 16 states across the northeastern U.S.
>
> The invasive bugs can wreak havoc on plants and trees and could eventually threaten the American wine industry as they develop into vibrant moth-like insects.

The spotted lanternfly, which can fly and is a plant-hopping insect, is believed to have arrived in the U.S. on a stone shipment from China in 2012, according to the New York State Integrated Pest Management Program at Cornell University in Ithaca.

The life cycle of the spotted lanternfly begins in mid-spring. They are closely related to the Cicadas family and primarily live in trees. The insects consume the sap of up to 70 different plant species during their life cycle, particularly fruit trees. As they eat, they release a sticky, sugary substance called honeydew that increases the growth of mold and attracts wasps and ants. Too much of the bugs feeding can weaken the tree and ultimately cause it to die."

It would stand to further reason that homeopathic health remedies that rely on natural foods and plant-based therapies will also be in short supply and won't be available to help the dying, therefore, increasing death tolls.

The final weapon that remains to kill will be with the beasts of the earth. This is by far the strangest of all the weapons each of the riders use to slay their prey. Do these beasts somehow lose control and wildly attack densely populated areas or maybe particularly only the rural populations? This weapon does not follow the possible natural progression of the previous severe calamities. In times of war, famine and disease naturally lead to depopulation and upset the balance between human civilization and wildlife. If hunting and developing of wilderness areas are diminished or eliminated, the population of predatory creatures could increase the chance of animal attacks. Exodus Chp.23 v.29 (KJV) says,

> "I will not drive them out from before thee in one year; lest the **land become desolate**, and the **beasts of the field multiply against thee.**"
> (Emphasis mine).

The word *beasts* in this verse is translated from the Greek word *thirio* which means *wild*. Because the Bible says *beasts of the field*, we would render that phrase to be *wild animals*. The word *wild animals* translated from the Greek word *therion* often means a *savage* or *poisonous animal*. There are over 2.13 million species of animals on the Earth. It is interesting to note that the animals that will kill the remaining 500 million people are the poisonous ones. We are not necessarily looking for wild animals that will be killing 500 million humans by a direct attack through fierce stings, piercing claws, or ravenous bites, but perhaps by the poison the animals will carry within their body. With this translation, the verse did not say diseased animals. It said poisonous animals. The only way for a toxic animal to affect a human is if the human eats the animal. The familiar adage, *you are what you eat,* comes to mind. I heard Dr. Steven Gundry, a famous American Heart Surgeon and best-selling author, once say,

> "You are what you eat, but more so, you are what the thing you're eating ate."

According to the Global Salmon Initiative (GSI),

> "One of the biggest evolutions in salmon feed is a decrease in fish-based ingredients and an

increase in plant-based ingredients, like algae or canola oil. **Soy, wheat, corn, peas and beans** are also used as plant-based protein alternatives." (Emphasis mine).

Soy, wheat, corn, peas and beans would never be found or eaten by salmon in the Pacific or North Atlantic Basin. Those kinds of filler substances are not part of their natural habitat. An online article by Family Friendly Farms discussed the danger soy and corn-fed animals have on consumers,

> "Consuming meat from animals raised on corn and soy diets brings the health concerns of these animals to our dinner tables. This transfer of health issues poses risks to human consumers…Meat from animals fed predominantly on corn and soy may lack essential nutrients, leading to potential nutrient deficiencies in humans who consume such meat…The use of antibiotics in animal agriculture can result in the presence of antibiotic residues in meat. When humans consume such meat, they may unwittingly expose themselves to these residues, contributing to antibiotic resistance and further contamination of the human nervous system with these foreign substances…Corn-fed animals tend to produce meat with an imbalance of omega-6 to omega-3 fatty acids. Excessive consumption of omega-6 fatty acids has been linked to inflammation and chronic diseases in humans…Excessive consumption of corn and soy in processed foods can contribute to obesity and metabolic syndrome due to their high caloric content and impact on

insulin resistance…Just as in animals, humans can develop allergies to corn and soy, leading to allergic reactions and digestive sensitivities."

Could it be that the ingestion of animals being fed erroneous fillers to fatten them up, which will undoubtedly lead the human body to massive nutritional deficiencies from pernicious meat eating, will be a dreadful cause of mass death?

You are considered to have been poisoned if anything you swallow, inhale, or touch subsequently causes you to become sick. A further concern regarding the diet of the animals we eat is the multiple types of contamination and sprays various livestock are exposed to that taints their food. This could come from toxic plants, insecticides, herbicides, lead, moldy hay, frost-stressed plants, and vermin poisons to name a few. An animal can become deadly to its consumer when it ingests poisons in multiple ways. The Environmental Working Group (EWG) on May 22, 2022, published a digital article written by Scott Faber who said,

> "The number of U.S. food manufacturing facilities inspected each year by the Food and Drug Administration has fallen by thousands over the last decade, despite Congress creating a mandate to increase inspections."

It is by no stretch of the imagination that the food supply could purposely become poisoned giving way to more deceptive ecological farming friendly green new deals geared more towards controlling and enslaving a free people. News 18 put out an article on February 18, 2021, that was curated by Raka Mukerjee regarding Bill Gates' idea on how to address climate change,

> "Billionaire and philanthropist, Bill Gates has a solution to the impending climate change disaster: Switch to synthetic meat.
>
> The billionaire American business magnet, software developer, and philanthropist has a new book out, called 'How to Avoid a Climate Disaster.' One of his **top solutions involved synthetic meat.** 'I do think all rich countries should move to 100% synthetic beef, Gates said in an interview with MIT TECHNOLOGY REVIEW, on how **to cut back on methane emissions.** "You can get used to the taste difference, and the claim is they're going to make it taste even better over time. Eventually, that **green premium** is modest enough that you can sort of **change the people** or **use regulation** to totally shift the demand." (Emphasis mine).

There are over two million farms in the United States. More than half the nation's land is used for agriculture. The number of farms within America have declined since the 1930s. Agriculture extends into industries such as food service and food manufacturing. It will be climate change and green policy making that will truly lead to the detriment of the global food chain supply. California is a prime example of how government can negatively affect agriculture, which can be seen through their forced water shortages. California's water board agencies like to blame climate change for the lack of available water; however, on January 13, 2023, Breanna Polk and Amy Pachla reported on ABC 23 News that,

"BAKERSFIELD, Calif. (KERO) — California has seen heavy rainfall over the past few weeks, but nearly all the water collected in the Sacramento-San Joaquin Delta was dumped into the ocean, leaving farmers in the Central Valley with questions and concerns.

Farmers like Jason Giannelli, who say the rainfall they receive throughout the year is always helpful for growing crops like processing tomatoes, almonds, pistachios and more. However, one thing he says farmers are concerned about is water storage.

According to Giannelli, who is a fourth-generation family farmer here in Kern, the pumps running from the delta to the aqueduct are only operating at about 20 percent capacity, with the majority of the water being flushed out into the ocean.

'We are talking about a national security issue when you think about it, because Kern County alone is the number one [food] producing county in the country. Give us our water and you wouldn't have a sigma problem or anything like that. They want to claim overdraft and everything else, but it's not because we have an overdraft problem. We have an over-regulation problem, and we're not getting our water,' said Giannelli.

The 'California Department of Water Resources' says the Sacramento-San Joaquin Delta is the hub of California's water supply, providing fresh water to two-thirds of the state's population, and to millions of acres of farmland.

With 95 percent of the water going from the delta directly back into the ocean, Giannelli says the issue at hand is simple: Regulation."

California's purposeful water debacle shows how sold-out legislators control of the food chain supply can be dominated and purposely over-regulated under the foolish precept of safeguarding the environment in exchange for a deceptive eco-friendly green planet agenda.

Another argument that is in support of the ideology of a greener planet was made by The Smithsonian Magazine's Daily Correspondent Margaret Osborne on July 14, 2023, who wrote,

"More than half of the world's oceans have changed significantly in color over the past 20 years, with **climate change** as the likely cause, new research suggests. Oceans around the equator **have shifted** to **a greener hue**, a trend that cannot be explained by natural, year-to-year variability alone...Bluer oceans tend to have little life, while greener oceans have more phytoplankton— marine algae that photosynthesize. Phytoplankton are the base of the marine food web, serving as fuel for zooplankton and fish, which in turn are eaten by larger fish, seabirds and marine mammals. But phytoplankton are also critical for combating the climate crises. Researchers estimate the oceans absorb about 30% of carbon dioxide produced by humans, largely thanks to the photosynthesis of these algae. Different kinds of plankton reflect and absorb light in different ways, meaning that a shifting ocean color equates to a changing ecosystem…To determine whether the trend was related to **climate change**, the team, B.B. Caelan ocean and climate scientist at the National Oceanography Center in England and his colleagues, turned to a model created by study co-author Stephanie Dutkiewicz in 2019, which simulated how the Earth's oceans would respond under two scenarios: one with added greenhouse gases and one without. The results predicted in the **greenhouse** gas model aligned almost exactly with what the researchers found from real-world data—within 20 years, about half of the oceans significantly shifted in color, per the MIT statement." (Emphasis mine).

Personally, I do not believe in climate change as the current narrative would have you perceive it. I remember in 1987, the news announcing that there was a hole in the ozone layer and we were no longer going to be protected from the sun's rays. As a result, in just a few short years, we were all going to burn up and die if we didn't stop using aerosol hairspray cans. That didn't happen. In 1989, the greatest of the U.N. scientists predicted that global warming if left unchecked would cause coastal cities to be underwater by the year 2000. Well, here we are now in 2024 and that also didn't happen. Another over politicized geological scientific group in 2018 made a claim that after the 1994 Northridge earthquake, California should have already had the "big one." Apparently, California is way overdue for a "big one." Al Gore with his documentary movie, "An Inconvenient Truth," predicted in 2007 that by 2013 the

Arctic Ocean would be completely ice free. That didn't happen either. At some point in time, we need to stop politicizing science. Rep. Alexandria Ocasio-Cortez, D-N.Y., said the world has 12 years before it ends if we don't address climate change. Being a believer in the Lord Jesus Christ, I'm sure He'd like to know how she came up with that number when God the Father didn't tell His Son nor the angels when Heaven and Earth would end.

One potential sinister plot that may already be in motion are the conspiracy theories surrounding chemtrails. Every person I've spoken to in California, irrelevant of chosen party, have all looked at the sky and admitted they've witnessed crisscross patterns of white trails that begin early in the morning and last throughout the day. Many have said how those chemtrails eventually block out the sun and turn what would have been a bright warm sunny day into a hazy gloomy day. They also make the naturally orangish-yellow sun turn into a white appearing sun. In fact, many have noted that the haze in the trails appear to be layered with multi-colored luminescence that magnifies the sun's glare. According to sky observers, the white cloudy grids in our beautiful blue skies may contain chemicals and other potential biologic agents that may be dropping hazardous poisons and possibly various technologies into our environment. It is a heinous agenda that may lead to warmer temperatures and dryer vegetation and crops. Many conspiracy theorists claim the chemtrails are administered by a cabal that is scheming to depopulate the masses. They say each day that they grid our sky is providing another opportunity for a beta-test in preparation for when these ingloriously wicked people will decide to proliferate their villainy.

Climate change, climate catastrophe, climate inaction, climate crisis, global warming, global boiling, environmental destruction, environmental collapse, weather destabilization, going green, and green new deals are nothing more than emotional attention phrase grabbers designed to fear monger free people into a central global governance rift with evil perpetrators.

In August 2014, Climate Change was given a logo. The logo is a plain green and black circle. The circle is brightest and greenest at the bottom and darkens into pure black at the top. "The logo represents Earth, with the bright green symbolizing life and the smoky black showing the deadly effects of climate change," according to the logo creator Milton Glaser. Global Alliance for a Green New Deal uses a spiraled circle layered logo. California's Green New Deal Coalition uses the outline of the state and colors it green with green bolded letters as their logo. Green New Deal Devon uses a green double speared stick drawn green arrow pointing upward and several more across every nation. The color of the pale green horse matches the area of industry of the green new deal and climate change logos. This area of enterprise aims to obtain full dominion over the entire planet's eco-agriculture system that will bring a worldwide calamitous death toll. This jurisdictional supremacy armada is strategically moving in a position so that the *sons of disobedience* can engage in a vicious ecological false flag.

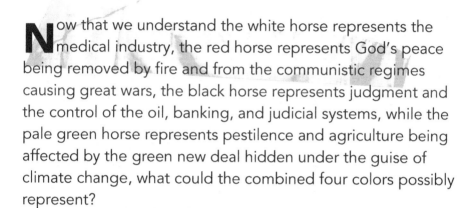

CHAPTER 20

WHITE, RED, BLACK, and GREEN

N ow that we understand the white horse represents the medical industry, the red horse represents God's peace being removed by fire and from the communistic regimes causing great wars, the black horse represents judgment and the control of the oil, banking, and judicial systems, while the pale green horse represents pestilence and agriculture being affected by the green new deal hidden under the guise of climate change, what could the combined four colors possibly represent?

The colors white, red, black, and green are predominantly associated with the Pan-Islamism or Pan-Arab Muslim nations. According to their own history, the meaning and symbolism behind those colors are found in the succession of Islamic Caliphates,

> "**Black** represents the Rashidun caliphate, which existed from 632-661, and the Abbasid Caliphate, which existed from 750-1517. These are the first and third true Caliphates respectively, and they were marked by a pure black banner. The color **white** represents the second Caliphate, the Umayyad Caliphate, which was the true Caliphate from 661-750, and whose banner color was white. The color **green** represents the Fatimid Caliphate,

which existed from 909-1171 in North Africa
before being conquered by the Abbasids. **Red**
represents the Hashemites, who have traditionally
ruled Mecca, and the Ottomans, who, while not
Arab, were the fourth true Caliphate and
controlled many Arab lands." (Emphasis mine).

Since the October 7, 2023, Hamas led-attack on Israel, Palestinians have taken to the streets engaged in riots, vandalism, and assaults. In the act of defiance, they have removed other nation's flags in the countries where they reside and have replaced them with their own flag. This is especially seen in America. To allow for their nation's flag to be raised above or in place of the American flag on our soil symbolizes that we are allowing for the abduction and seizing of our country. Their white, red, black, and green flag never bled for the United States. As a veteran, that undermines everything that I fought for, what I risked my life to protect, and what every other American service member ever sacrificed to defend.

Symbols have meaning and since the inception of the United States, America has never had any other flag raised above or in place of its own for any reason. Historically, Islam has always been spread by way of conquest. In order for there to be a call to jihad (holy war) one such criteria is that it must be in defense of Allah. It allows Muslims to fight those who fight them. The majority of Muslims around the world believe Israel has oppressed and attacked their people for far too long. According to prophetic tradition (Hadith), the black flag was the battle flag of the Prophet Muhammed and carried into battle by many of his companions. The image of the black flag has been used as a symbol of religious revolt and engagement in battle. Contemporary Islamist movements use the black flag with the shahada to evoke notions of jihad and of reestablishing the Islamic Caliphate. It's possible that a unified white, red, black, and green flag will be the final standing centrifuge symbol to evoke a world Islamist holy war that would also signify the possible appearance and descendant of Muhammed, *Muhammed al-Mahdi*.

Muslims are waiting for their *Mahdi*, the rightly guided one, who is a future final leader according to Islam eschatology who will appear during the end of days and purge the world of evil and corruption. This sounds eerily similar to the teachings of the Christians and Jews. The Muslim's *Mahdi* and the Bible's description of the Antichrist are incredibly similar in nature in regards to when they are to appear, the length of time they are granted power over the world, and what they are to accomplish. First, the Bible says that the tribulation will last for seven years and Islam claims that the Twelfth Imam, Mahdi, will rule the world for the same amount of time. Second, Muslims anticipate three years of chaos before the revealing of the Twelfth Imam and the Bible speaks of three and a half years of tribulation before the Antichrist reveals his true nature by desecrating the Jewish temple also known as the Desolation of Abomination. Third, the Bible describes the Antichrist as a deceiver who claims to bring peace, but who actually brings widespread war and the expectation of the Twelfth Imam is that he will bring peace through massive war with the entire world.

In the not-too-distant past, people of many nations thought that the Antichrist was Nero, Hitler, Arafat, Khaddafi, Gorbachev, or Pope John Paul II. All of these men are dead today. If one of them had truly been the Antichrist, we would have to be living in the millennial time with Christ. The Antichrist clearly has not yet come. I do believe the Antichrist will rise out of the sea of the Middle Eastern people through politics or as a political figure. I do believe he will also be a westernized Muslim. I do not believe Islam itself to be the beast, but rather Islam is the catapult that will have a hand in the charge of the beast through beheadings. Revelation Chp.20 v.4 (KJV) says,

> "And I saw thrones, and they sat upon them, and judgment was given unto them: and I saw the souls of them **that were beheaded** for the **witness of Jesus,** and for the word of God, and which had not worshipped the beast, neither his image, neither had received his mark upon their foreheads, or in their hands; and they lived and reigned with Christ a thousand years. (Emphasis mine).

Who will be the enforcers that are given power over those who will not worship the beast or his image and who will be the one's beheaded for the witnessing of Christ? It is possible that they will be the Muslim Jihadists. Jihadists are notorious for cutting off the heads of their captives in order to strike fear into their enemies. The Muslim call to jihad is cemented within the Qur'an and is clearly present from the beginning of Islamic history, written in their scripture, never to be separated from their zeal, and in the life of the Prophet (*Hadith*).

The Qur'an discusses beheadings in two surahs that provide justification for them in Chp.8 v.12 which states,

> "When the Lord inspired the angels (saying) I am with you. So, make those who believe stand firm. I will throw fear into the hearts of those who disbelieve. **Then smite the necks** and smite of

208

them each finger." (Emphasis mine).

The Qur'an also says in Chp. 47 v. 4,

> "Now when ye meet in battle those who
> disbelieve, **then it is smiting of the necks** until,
> when ye have routed them, making fast of bonds;
> and afterward either grace or ransom 'til the war
> lay down its burdens." (Emphasis mine).

This practice remains active in present day Saudi Arabia and is a concept widely practiced by all Muslim extremist groups who are spread out across all nations. No other religion permits the smiting of necks the way the Qur'an does. There is an argument that most Muslims have done away with this barbaric practice, renouncing violence, but that would mean that those Muslims have turned away from the true teachings of Islam and fail to fully embrace their faith in Allah.

The correlation between the Islamic and Christian beheadings cannot be overlooked. The phrase *Allahu Akbar* in Islam translates to *God is Greater*. One must ask, greater than who, greater than what? The God of the Bible in Exodus Chp.3 v.14 (NKJV) says,

> "And God said to Moses, '**I AM WHO I AM**.' And
> He said, 'Thus you shall say to the children of
> Israel, **I AM** has sent me to you.'" (Emphasis
> mine).

One of the gods appears to have the need to justify or compare their greatness. The other God simply states, "I AM." This means He is the absolute of *all*. He exists in and of Himself. The statement of *I AM* tells me there must be an inconsistency within the writings of Islam as to who is the true God of gods.

I find it most peculiar that the name of Jesus (*Isa*), Jesus son of Mary (*Maryam*), His titles, and His attributes are mentioned one hundred and eight times in ninety-three verses of the Qur'an. He is called the Spirit of God seven different times and is one of the six prophets given a holy title. Adam was titled, *the Chosen of God*. Noah, *the Preacher for God*. Abraham, *the Friend of God*. Moses, *the Speaker with God*. JESUS, *THE WORD OF GOD*. Muhammad, *the Apostle of God*. It is not a coincidence that they give Jesus the title of *the Word of God*. The Bible describes Jesus in John Chp.1 v.1 (ESV) when John writes,

> "In the beginning was **the Word**, and **the Word** was with God, and **the Word was God**." (Emphasis mine).

Muslims believe that Jesus (Eisa) will return at the end of days as the Sunnah, Islamic traditions and practices, as narrated by Abu Hurairah that the Prophet said,

> "The Hour will not begin until **Jesus**, son of Mary, (**Eisa** bin Maryam) comes down as a just judge and a just ruler. He will break the cross, kill the pigs and abolish Jizyah (tax). Then there will be abundance of money and nobody will accept charitable gifts."

Sadly in 2023, Hamas launched their horrific surprise attack upon an unsuspecting innocent people of Israel. Reported over several Israeli news media and online article news outlets, the conflict began a month prior to the October's sneak attack portraying armed Hamas terrorists breaching the border security fence that separates Gaza from Israel. Social media lit up with videos showing Hamas terrorists gunning down Israeli civilians of all ages indiscriminately on the open streets and in their homes. Further reports were made about soldiers being caught off-guard and attacked on military bases. National headlines proclaimed that militants brought death from the sky paragliding into Israel unleashing their brutality at an open-air music festival upon a large crowd of unarmed civilians. Rumors revealed that possible *beheadings* of the innocent that were captured followed their assault. Palestinians and sympathizers are claiming justification for their attacks citing Israel is engaging in genocide and has been for decades.

I was born in the 70's and there was never a time outside of World War II with the holocaust that stretched between 1939-1945 that I can recall where anti-Semitism was at an all-time high like it is today. Every government is purposely or ignorantly uniting in what appears to be a future siege against Israel. The re-emergence of the hatred for Jews is what has pulled sympathizing nations together and will potentially lead to a World War III against the nation of Israel. A united world Caliphate might be the trigger or movement that ignites a global jihad.

Deuteronomy Chp.28 v.49 (NIV) says,

> "The Lord will bring **a nation against** you from far away, from the ends of the earth, **like an eagle** swooping down, a nation whose language you will

not understand." (Emphasis mine).

The *eagle* has always represented America since America's formation. Sadly, America is not mentioned in Revelation. Westerners tend to forget the Bible is a Middle Eastern book. I believe this verse not only is in reference to the most ancient Babylonian monarchy that began during the time of Nimrod and spoke the language of Syriac, but is a possible indication and foreshadowing that America, a distant land, is a key factor or co-factor in the initiation of all nations rising against the Jews. Furthermore, Zechariah Chp.12 v.2-4 (ESV) prophesies,

> "Behold, I am about to make Jerusalem a cup of staggering to all the surrounding peoples. **The siege** of Jerusalem will also be against Judah. On that day I will make Jerusalem **a heavy stone** for all the peoples. All who lift it will surely hurt themselves. And **all the nations of the earth will gather against it**. On that day, declares the LORD, **I will strike every** horse with **panic**, and its rider with **madness**. But for the sake of the house of Judah I will keep my eyes open, when I strike every horse of the peoples with **blindness**." (Emphasis mine).

The word *all* means every single nation on the Earth will come against Israel. Israel is a nation the size of New Jersey. Because I am a believer in the Bible, I would never attack a nation when God clearly says He will strike the assaulting nation that comes against her with *panic, madness,* and *blindness.* I can't imagine the awesome power that will be wielded to prevent Israel's destruction. Sadly, many will fail to heed His warnings spoken in prophecy that they should not attack Israel.

Many would ask, what's so important about Israel? I'll be honest, when I was in the Middle East, I couldn't wait to leave. The majority of that area is a desert oasis of burning oil refineries. The stench of sulfur from the desert fields of oil rigs never departs the air and spreads across the region for hundreds of miles. When I served my tours and was overseas in the Middle East during the summer, the temperatures rose as high as 135 degrees in the day and was no cooler than 90 degrees at night. The constant sand storms left a crunch in every bite of food I ate. The primary reason the world is fighting over that geographical area is because it is considered the cradle of civilization. It is also the dawning location of the three most influential major monotheistic religions.

Another strange but noteworthy reason for why Israel is so important is that if you believe in a round, blue, and spherical Earth as depicted in a T and O map also known as an *Isidore* map, Jerusalem is at the center of the Earth. If you believe in the flat Earth model as depicted in a series of medieval Christian maps like the Hereford Mappa Mundi which is best known for depicting the world as a circular flat landmass surrounded by ocean and a circular ice wall, Jerusalem is also seen at the center of the Earth. The Book of Jubilees written between 135-105 B.C. mentions Mount Zion as the *naval* of the Earth,

> "And he (Noah) knew that the Garden of Eden is the holy of holies and the Lord's dwelling place, and Mount Sinai the center of the desert, and Mount Zion the center of **the navel** of the Earth." (Emphasis mine).

The world is being pulled to the very center of the Middle East conflict that has been going on since before you and I were even born. We are closely approaching the apex of this conflict that will thrust every nation to choose a side.

It took approximately three years from the time the white horse began its cantor to the time it gained control over the entire world. It would be a fair assumption that it would take three years for the red horse to accomplish its purpose as well. If each horse follows the same pattern of time, we must conclude that by 2032 all four horsemen will be in full gallop and the world will be in utter chaos. That year is formidably close to the United Nations 2030 Agenda of Sustainable Development. This is not a prediction, but merely an observation.

Do not be discouraged. I am always reminded of one particular verse that keeps me fighting to change things for the better from 2 Chronicles Chp.7 v.14 (NIV) that says,

> "If my people, who are called by my name, will
> humble themselves and pray and seek my
> face and **turn from their wicked ways**, then I will
> hear from heaven, and I will **forgive** their **sin** and
> **will heal their land.**" (Emphasis mine).

I firmly believe we are not out of the fight just yet and that we still have enough time and the ability to *humble* ourselves, *pray, seek,* and *turn* from the vile we've come to normalize. If we do those things, He can and will heal our land. It's time to stand up, voice up, and fight back!

We can confirm that we are indeed approaching the end of days because Mathew Chp.24 v.32-35 (NLT) tells us,

"Now learn a lesson from the **fig tree**. When its branches **bud** and its leaves begin to sprout, you know that summer is near. In the same way, when you see all these things, you can know **his return is very near**, right at the door. I tell you the truth, this **generation** will not pass from the scene until all these things take place. Heaven and earth will disappear, but my words will never disappear." (Emphasis mine).

The *fig tree* represents Israel and that the generation that sees Israel *bud* or come back to life will not pass. Israel's branch has already become tender and put forth leaves. The generation that witnesses all of this is not supposed to pass away until Jesus returns. Many biblical scholars have debated over what the Bible describes the timeframe of a generation to be. Most agree that a generation is 40 years, but the Bible uses several ways to describe what constitutes the time of a generation. In my opinion, Psalms Chp.90 v.10 (NKJV) stands out above all and says,

"The days of our lives are **seventy years**;
And if by reason of **strength they are eighty years**,
Yet their boast is only labor and sorrow;
For it is soon cut off, and we fly away." (Emphasis mine).

If we are to adhere to the prescribed notion of a generation constituting 40 years, this verse tells me that one generation can expand by strength through another generation. This would indicate more than one generation will see the return of Jesus. 80 years from the time that Israel was re-established as a nation in 1948 would be 2028. Because most nations no longer use the biblical Hebrew calendar and instead use the Gregorian calendar, we know that Satan has already changed *the times* as he did *the laws* spoken about in Daniel so that we would be unprepared to watch for His return.

2028 to 2032 is not a prediction, but as a Watchman on the wall it is simply an observation of a time to pay attention. There are many factors and prerequisites that need to happen before then. With so many signs in the heavens and the unhinged times we are living in, I believe it to be very possible that Jesus, King of Kings, is coming back and the Baby Boomers, Gen X, Gen Y (Millennials), Gen Z, and Gen Alpha are the last and final living generations who may very well be blessed to witness His return in these final days. We may be THIS generation that shall not pass before His return!

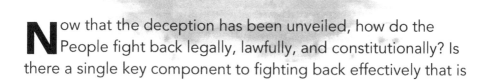

CHAPTER 21

FIGHT BACK

Now that the deception has been unveiled, how do the People fight back legally, lawfully, and constitutionally? Is there a single key component to fighting back effectively that is tangible before the possibility of another American civil war or worse, a world war?

Everything starts with the oath. In the United States and all nation states that make up America, people who decide to take up the mantle and protect our freedoms shall swear or affirm their oath before entering upon the duties of their respective offices according to the U.S. Constitution and their state constitutions. Everything stems from the oath because it is binding. At least, it is supposed to be. It is the one accountable and self-accountable tool that is used to ensure elected representatives who step into their positions never cleave into becoming your leader, but are demanded to render themselves as a servant of their constituents with only one real power granted by the consent of the governed. They are to secure the rights of the People by supporting, upholding, and defending the Supreme Law of the Land even at the expense of their very life if it is ever called upon. It is written in the Declaration of Independence,

> "...that to **Secure these Rights**, Governments are instituted among Men, deriving their **just Powers**

from the **consent of the governed.**" (Emphasis mine).

I've listened to many businessowners, parents, and various concerned individuals scream their redress of grievances at their board of supervisors, city councils, mayors, legislators, sheriffs, and even the governor that they are violating their oath and are duty bound to defend the very public they swore to protect. If the People's outrage and injustices are based in truth, then what are the communities to do when moral obligation is barren within their government institutions? What are we all missing?

Since every state has their own oath of office that inescapably *shall* be administered to every would-be government official, we must first understand and become familiar with what is written within that oath. California's present-day oath is one of the longest and most unyielding. It states in paragraph one,

> "I, _____, do solemnly swear (or affirm) that I will **support** and **defend** the Constitution of the United States and the Constitution of the State of California against **all** enemies, foreign and **domestic**; that I will bear true faith and allegiance to the **Constitution of the United States** and the **Constitution of the State of California**; that I take this obligation freely, without any mental reservation or purpose of evasion; and that I will well and faithfully discharge the duties upon which I am about to enter." (Emphasis mine).

This first paragraph to California's oath of office appears to be simple in nature and easy to understand. Though the first paragraph appears to be binding and stacked to ensure acts of good fidelity, it is without answerability. We must ask what constitutes accountability or liability for a violation of that sworn oath?

We have established that the United States is a corporation and not a government. At the end of the Civil War, congress reconvened and passed what was called the United States Reorganization Act of 1871 also known as the Act to Provide a Municipal Government for the District of Columbia. This new government was different. It was structured as a foreign owned corporation and suspiciously also named the UNITED STATES. This undoubtedly was designed to cause confoundment because it adopted the republic constitution, but it changed one word. This new UNITED STATES *corporation* changed the word Constitution *FOR* the United States to the Constitution *OF* the UNITED STATES. This made the constitution a possession of a de-facto government and no longer the possession of the People. The chosen words matter. Also, in the first paragraph of California's oath of office, it uses the word *OF* instead of *FOR* which is why the People of California in 1951 imposed under proposition 6 an amendment to the oath. It was amended on November 4, 1952, with a second paragraph to ensure the rights of the People would not be undermined by any subversive tactics.

In the second paragraph of California's oath of office, it currently reads,

> "And I do further swear (or affirm) that **I do not advocate**, nor am I a member of any party or organization, political or **otherwise**, that **now advocates** the overthrow of the Government of

the United States or of the State of California by force or violence or **other unlawful means**; that within the five years immediately preceding the taking of this oath (or affirmation) I have not been a member of any party or organization, political or **otherwise, that advocated** the overthrow of the Government of the United States or of the State of California by force or violence or **other unlawful means** except as follows:

(If no affiliations, write in the words "No Exceptions")_____
and that during such time as I hold the office of _____ (name of office)

I will not advocate nor become a member of any party or organization, political or **otherwise**, that **advocates** the overthrow of the Government of the United States or of the State of California by force or violence or **other unlawful means**." (Emphasis mine).

This second paragraph was designed to ensure that if anyone was voted in by the People, those elected officers were to be of sound character not ever having supported seditious ideologies evident through having *advocated* in the past or present for the overthrow of the United States or State of California's government by an *otherwise* or *other unlawful means* nor would they commit this in the future. This was beautifully drafted. Its primary function was to prevent infiltration of communists and other incendiary factions into local and state government.

Anti-Communist fervor reached new heights during the early 1950s. Senator Joseph McCarthy lead the charge against communism which inundated national media headlines causing American panic. The federal government imprisoned communist leaders under the Smith Act and passed a rigid law called the McCarran Act also known as the Internal Security Act of 1950. This law required the registration of organizations and their officers and members as communist-action, communist-front, or communist-infiltrated. America's nationwide *Red Scare* accelerated the hunt and expulsion of any and all anti-capitalist sympathizers. The fear was that communists could be infiltrating anywhere using their positions as labor organizers, artists, journalists, college professors, and school teachers to aid their programs and propaganda of world communist indoctrination and domination. This fear led to the Communist Control Act of 1954 that was signed into law by President Eisenhower which prohibited members of Communist organizations from serving in certain representative capacities. Communist party members were then forced to seek asylum in murky obscure areas within American society, if they could find it.

An *otherwise* body or organization was the umbrellaed word that aimed to prevent any entity, irrelevant of how they appeared on the surface, who wanted to vitiate American governing authorities from doing so under any other *unlawful means. Other unlawful means* was the phrase to include all ruinous attempts regardless of how unintentional or impartial the act may appear. A key purpose behind phrasing the words *other unlawful means* was another way of preventing the tactics of Fabianism from gradually taking effect in American communities. As previously discussed, gradualism was predominantly orchestrated by means of egregious legislation.

The changing of the language to change perception to achieve their insidious goals.

The second paragraph of the oath prohibiting the affiliation with organizations advocating the overthrow of the government was struck down by the California Supreme Court as an unconstitutional infringement on 1st Amendment rights in **Vogel vs. County of Los Angeles** (1967), 68 Cal.2d 18 issued on December 21, 1967, and ending January 20, 1968. At present, only the first paragraph is administered for either the oath of office to officers, deputies, and or loyalty employees. California's State Constitution was never amended to reflect the ruling. However, both the first and the second paragraph were codified which is egregious. The trial ignored the power the People hold over the behavior of their elected officers. Whenever a person enters the employment of the state or any subdivision thereof, they voluntarily surrender certain rights, immunities, and status above government as a sovereign. They would maintain those rights only if they chose to negate their servantry. In accepting the oath, they are granted a position which places them under the Will of the People in exchange for becoming gatekeepers and guardians over all rights and privileges. They are willfully accepting that they no longer have full access to those rights and privileges while operating in the capacity of the duties of their respective position.

California's State Constitution is the highest authority of the state and must harmonize with the Supreme Law of the Land. If a trial jury found the second paragraph to be invalid because it infringed upon the 1st Amendment, the state legislature does not have the authority to codify it meaning to reduce a law that was amended in the state constitution into a code. Administering only the first paragraph of the oath bastardizes the proper oath set forth by the People. This was never approved. Failure to amend the oath after flagrant codification is willful complicity at best because the court ruling requires state representatives to amend the California State Constitution's oath properly. A codification uniforms a law by diminishing its authority to a state code. This undermines the Will of the People because the invalidation ruling was never publicly announced for nearly fifteen years after the oath's initial enactment. Proposition 6 was the People's authority to hold official representatives to severe consequences should they engage in an "otherwise…other unlawful means." Remember, our servants are only in their elected positions to secure the rights of the People and to stay within the confines and the limitation of powers outlined in both the federal and all state constitutions. By codifying the first and second paragraph while leaving in the original oath unamended in the state constitution, it purposely creates ambiguity. American Jurisprudence reflects negatively on ambiguity because it places doubt in the court of public edict and restricts lawful enforcement upon intolerable behavior. Whenever ambiguity arises, a Maxum-of-Law must be recognized as was ruled in **Coffin v. Ogden** 85 U.S. 120, 124 that

> "(15d.) The law requires, not conjecture, but **certainty**." (Emphasis mine).

Obscuring the Vogel trial and failing to amend the oath caused havoc in the 2002 gubernatorial election in **Jesson vs. Davis** 97 Cal.App.4th 1032. The California Court of Appeal Fourth Appellate District upheld the injunction of paragraph two to the California oath of office. The court recognized Gubernatorial Candidate Nick Jesson's argument that the offending oath was required per the second paragraph found in Article XX. Sec. 3

to be signed by all candidates. It was also later acknowledged by the court that the previous Vogel trial ruling only applied to loyalty employees, not elected officials. However, the presiding judge, Judge John M. Watson, having found a similar case in Oklahoma ruled that the Vogel trial jury's final judgment can and will be applied in continuity to California's elected officials and candidate filings. For the second time, California representatives had failed to amend the oath.

The mere fact that the Court of Appeal recognized the Vogel trial had no effect on elected officials proves that all representatives who failed to file signed affirmation of both oath of office paragraphs between 1968 and 2002 entered upon their duties illegally. That includes all officials from all branches of government in California. The seats at those times were technically vacant. Every act thereof by those officials from any branch must be stricken from the books and nullified, effective immediately. Judge Watson would not have wanted to go down a road that could have unraveled a slew of egregious legislation and rulings, including his own, along with possible false incarcerations and imprisonments. Their argument to solidify continuity was lack of supporting distinction between non-elected and elected state employees. This rationale was based off of a decision similar to **Wieman v. Updegraff** (1952), 344 U.S. 183 which struck down an Oklahoma loyalty oath required of *all state officers*. We read in the court transcript that it was litigated in light of the oath's purpose of making,

> "**loyalty** a qualification to hold public office or be employed by the State." (Emphasis mine)

In the case of **Jesson v. Davis**, the ruling flagrantly undermined the Supreme Law of the Land because the U.S. Constitution in Article VI. Paragraph 3 says,

> "The Senators and Representatives before mentioned, and the Members of the several State Legislatures, and all executive and judicial Officers, both of the United States and of the several States, **shall be bound by Oath or Affirmation**, to support this Constitution; but no religious Test shall ever be required as a Qualification to any Office or public Trust under the United States." (Emphasis mine).

Clearly the oath is a bond, an *allegiance* to the Constitution and the state constitution. The word *allegiance* is written in the first paragraph of the oath. One cannot fulfill the obligation to that oath if they have no *allegiance* meaning *loyalty* to secure the rights of the People in the first place. The word *loyalty* is a synonym for *faithfulness*. The word *faithfully* is also written in the first paragraph of the oath. If the argument was based on the premise that loyalty was not a requirement to hold public office or be employed by the state than both paragraphs should have been ruled invalidated. Instead, the Judge and the Court of Appeals decided to cherry pick. They were wrong. Loyalty, faithfulness, and allegiance after one's affirmation becomes a bond and is, therefore, a demand. The oath is the binding contract between the servant of the People that *shall* be administered according to the state constitution. Without it, what is the point of having the oath?

The court also purposely skirted around the phrasing of *otherwise* and *other unlawful means*. Because the court disregarded those umbrellaed phrases, it opened up pandora's box for communist tactics to re-infiltrate our government by way of gradualism. True servants of the People would have amended the oath. California has a few ways that an amendment could have been made to eliminate such confoundment. So, why was there such a monumental failure to amend the oath? After all, codes must be uniform with the state constitution to provide a maxim of certainty. The answer is that ambiguity impedes justifiable prosecution because California government codes section 1368, 1369, 3108, and 3109 say with certainty that

> "Every person after having taken and subscribed to the oath or affirmation, any material matter later found to be false, engaging in an **otherwise, other unlawful means, is guilty of perjury, and guilty of felony**, and is **punishable by imprisonment** in the state prison for 2, 3, or 4 years pursuant to subdivision (h) of Section 1170 of the California Penal Code." (Emphasis mine).

The first reason why shameless servants of the People of California don't amend the oath is because of the government codes 1368, 1369, 3108, and 3109. The only prosecutorial effect for a violation of one's oath of office is through Paragraph 2. While it remains under codification, there is no consequence or punishment for the official because the state illegally no longer administers the second paragraph.

The second reason is because Black's Law Dictionary in the 11th Edition defines the word *discharge* as written in Paragraph 1 of the California State Constitution's oath of office as,

> "to **cancel** or unloose the obligation of a contract;

226

to make an **agreement** or **contract null and inoperative**." (Emphasis mine).

That means that any office holder who signs the oath of office with the word *discharge* written in the contract is canceling or nullifying and making inoperative any obligation they are affirming to uphold. In fact, the word *discharge* allows your representatives to engage in egregious behavior against their own constituents with impunity. This explains why malfeasance in government goes unchecked.

The third reason why California's State Constitution's oath of office has not been amended is the process by which it takes to amend it. California's State Constitution's first possible process for approving an amendment provides that the Legislature through a 2/3 vote propose an amendment or revision of the constitution. Each amendment is required to be prepared and submitted so that it can be voted on separately by the *electorate*. The second process to consent to an amendment specifies that the Legislature through a 2/3 vote submit at a general election the question whether to call a convention to revise the constitution. If the majority of the *electorate* votes yes, then within 6 months the Legislature is required to establish the Constitutional Convention. Delegates to a Constitutional Convention must be comprised of voters elected from districts in numbers equally representing the population in each district as may be practicable. The third process states that the *electors* may amend the constitution by initiative. The fourth method requires a proposed amendment or revision be submitted to the *electors*. If approved by a majority of votes, the revision takes effect on the fifth day after the Secretary of State files the statement of the vote for the election at which the measure was voted on, but the measure may provide that it becomes operative after its effective date. In all processes, amending California's oath of office would involve the *electors* and or the *electorate* which are the People. Present office holders choose to ignore amending the oath because it would require involving their constituents in order to necessitate an unparalleled, fixed oath free from invalidation and ensure accountability by imprisonment should representative officials ever engage in an *otherwise* or *other unlawful means* that would subvert the rights of the People when they currently have no such consequence for not upholding the duties of their office or protecting the rights of their constituents.

When California's representatives implemented statute 1369 back in 2011, it added criminal violation and punishment for any official regardless of which branch of government they were elected into who had taken the oath to a penitentiary. It states that,

> "Every person having taken and subscribed to the oath or affirmation required by this chapter, who while holding office, advocates or becomes a member of any party or organization, political or otherwise, that advocates the overthrow of the **government of the United States** by force or violence or other unlawful means, is guilty of a felony, and is punishable by **imprisonment** in the **state prison**." (Emphasis mine).

This code is nearly identical to the second paragraph of California's oath of office with one very important distinction. After the phrase "...government of the United States...," it left out, "or the State of California." This is another act of chicanery. California is part of the Union and is, therefore, a part of the United States government. On a surface level, this code would seem to apply to all California state officers, deputies, or loyalty employees; however, it does not. When California officials only sign the first paragraph to their oath of office, they have ignorantly and openly signed a cryptic and dubious contract. They are therefore under a contrasting and wretched jurisdiction outside the range of the People's authority. Since the right to a contract is not limited and the obligation cannot be prevented, the first paragraph of the California oath of office allows for flagitiously treacherous behavior. All officers, deputies, and loyalty employees are signing a defunct affirmation and cannot be held accountable for any illicit act or behavior that would be considered an *otherwise* or *other unlawful means*. Nonetheless, because they are signing a defunct oath, they are still in violation of the California State Constitution Article XX, Sec. 3 that states,

> "Members of the Legislature, and all public officers and employees, executive, legislative, and judicial, except such inferior officers and employees as may be by law exempted, **shall, before they enter** upon the duties of their respective offices, take and subscribe the following oath or affirmation." (Emphasis mine).

The word *shall* in law is an imperative action. The word *before* is an action performed *prior* to undertaking the duties of their respective offices. This confirms that anyone having subscribed to the defunct oath of office is illegally engaging in duties of the respective positions that are technically vacant. The signing of a defunct oath is criminal. The argument that representatives may have been unaware of the law is mute. After all, according to the judicial branch, *ignorantia juris non excusat* which translates from Latin to mean *ignorance of the law excuses not* and *ignorantia legis neminem excusat* which is Latin for *ignorance of law excuses no one*. These basic civic fundamentals, indicate that a person who is unaware of a law may not escape liability for violating that law merely because they are ignorant of its existence. Elected officials are no exception.

The United States Constitution emphasizes that if representatives fail to protect the Constitution of the United States, State, or Territory and do not honor their allegiance within a reasonable amount of time and this same overt act is witnessed by one or more individuals or within an open court, they are subject to felony treason, imprisonment, or possibly death. We read in the U.S. Constitution Article III. Sec. 3 that

> "Treason against the United States, shall consist only in **levying War** against them, or in adhering to their Enemies, giving them Aid and Comfort. No Person shall be convicted of Treason **unless on the Testimony of two Witnesses to the same overt Act,** or on Confession in open Court." (Emphasis mine).

United States Code; Title 18 (U.S.C.) Section 2381 also states that

> "Whoever, **owing allegiance** to the United States, **levies war** against them or **adheres to their enemies,** giving them aid and comfort within the United States or elsewhere, is **guilty of treason** and shall **suffer death, or imprisoned** and fined,

and **incapable of holding any U.S. office.**"
(Emphasis mine).

United States Code; Title 18 (U.S.C.) Section 2384 additionally declares that

> "**If two or more persons in any State** or **Territory,** or in any place subject to the jurisdiction of the United States, **conspire to overthrow, put down,** or to destroy by force the Government of the United States, or to levy war against them, or to **oppose** by force the authority thereof, or by force **to prevent, hinder, or delay the execution of any law of the United States,** or by force to seize, take, or possess any property of the United States contrary to the authority thereof, they shall each be fined under this title or **imprisoned** not more than twenty years, or both." (Emphasis mine).

You, the People, are the witnesses to subversive representatives levying acts against America. Whether they signed a scandalous oath or not, *the People* have witnessed their overt acts undermining the rights that have been endowed by the Creator. One of the most important actionable steps to fighting back that the People of California and the People of all other states can institute is through affirmative action. It applies to every state in the Union which would necessitate a superlative, uncompromising, rigid amended oath that harmonizes with the Constitution *for* the United States, the Supreme Law of the Land, and not the federal or state corporation which is free from liability.

Without credible representation grounded in His law, egregious legislation will continue to proliferate. Without dutiful executors who have the willingness to stand up in the face of adversity no matter the cost, criminality will run rampant. Without honorable jurors and magistrates, justice will never prevail. Without righteous knowledgeable communities, endowment of rights will cease to exist because freedom requires honorable sacrifice. The Will of the People and the rule of law is quickly becoming extinct.

I firmly believe that the oath of office in every state needs to be changed and placed on the next upcoming ballot by way of affirmative action to ensure the People maintain their status above government. The People need to permanently establish accountability by imprisonment for all government bodies, regardless of appointment, election, or by agency employment in order to protect their freedoms endowed by the Creator from a government that might fall victim to political whims or foreign manipulative regimes. The People need to remove all traces of possible ambiguity out of any oath that would be administered to a political official to prevent disgraceful agents from operating *wherever it's not said* and guarantee accountability through the contractual compulsion rendered by a fixed oath.

All oaths should be free from invalidation, subversion, and willful defiance. A possible draft of a revised oath should read as follows,

"I, _____, do solemnly swear (or affirm) that I will support, uphold, and defend the Constitution *for* the United States and the Constitution *for* the State of _____ against all enemies, foreign and domestic; that I will bear true faith, loyalty, and allegiance to the Constitution *for* the United States and the

Constitution *for* the State of _____; that I shall never engage in an otherwise, other unlawful means that would subvert, sabotage, or usurp the Constitution *for* the United States and the Constitution *for* the State of _____; and that I am subject to imprisonment shall I fail to secure Unalienable Rights above ALL; and that I knowingly and willingly take this obligation freely, without any mental reservation or purpose of evasion; and that I shall only execute the vested duties of _____, upon which I am about to enter, so help me God.

The People are almost at a point of no return. Amending our representative's oath of office is one of the few remaining peaceable options we have left to regain control over an uncouth, immoral, and malicious government.

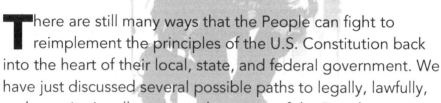

CHAPTER 22

WHEN ALL ELSE FAILS

There are still many ways that the People can fight to reimplement the principles of the U.S. Constitution back into the heart of their local, state, and federal government. We have just discussed several possible paths to legally, lawfully, and constitutionally activate the power of the People to peacefully correct the destructive path America is headed down.

Like my fellow brothers and sisters in arms, I have already put foot to ass for my country. I have proven myself with my very life. I owe nothing to no one. However, I did not want to stand silently by and watch all that I fought for and sacrificed to protect fall apart at the unchecked abuse of power within the branches of government and the slow detachment from the principles of the Constitution. This is why I have run for state governor in hopes of resetting what all free people are called to be...free!

I have frequently been asked, what would I do if I were elected as governor to end such emboldened villainy festering in all three branches? In short, I would begin with changing the oath of office for all elected officials to be held under imprisonment if they ever violated their sworn duty engaging in an *otherwise, other unlawful means*. I would then return California to a De Jure People's Grand Jury. Currently, America operates within the confines of a de facto corporation Grand Jury. Generally, a de facto Grand Jury is under the control of city district attorneys or county counsels and a judge or a local magistrate who administers authority through statutory law. However, it was the intention of our Forefathers to use a De Jure Grand Jury to ensure justice. Article 61 of the Magna Carta inspired our Founding Fathers to establish its presence in our Bill of Rights as a means to hold representatives accountable and allow for their removal by the People if they were to engage in criminality. Justice Antonin Scalia stated in the ruling of **United States v. Williams** (1992), 112 S.Ct. 1735, 504 U.S. 36, 118 L.Ed.2d 352 that

> "Our Founding Fathers presciently thereby created a 'buffer' the people may rely upon for justice, when public officials, including judges, criminally violate the law."

A De Jure People's Grand Jury functions under Common Law, His law, that which is endowed by the Creator and the authority vested within the constitution. Lastly, I would utilize a state military tribunal to hold California representatives culpable to their sedition as we are currently in a state of war because our country is being invaded by illegals due to the Biden Administration's *open border* policies that have caused illegal alien bombardment.

The U.S. Constitution in Article I. Sec. 10 says,

> "No State shall, without the Consent of Congress…keep Troops, or Ships of War in time of Peace…or engage in War, **unless actually invaded**, or

in such imminent Danger as will not admit of delay." (Emphasis mine).

In Article IV. Sec. 4 of the U.S. Constitution, it states,

> "**The United States** shall guarantee **to every State** in this Union a Republican Form of Government, and **shall protect each of them against Invasion**; and on Application of the Legislature, or of the Executive (when the Legislature cannot be convened) **against domestic Violence**." (Emphasis mine).

The U.S. Constitution has said that, "unless actually invaded, the United States to every State, shall protect each of them against Invasion." As a governor, it would be my sworn duty to protect the People within my state from an invasion. An invasion is defined by the American Heritage Dictionary of the English Language, 5th Edition as

> "an **intrusion** or encroachment. The act of **invading** a country or territory as an enemy; **hostile entrance** or intrusion. The act of invading; the act of **encroaching** upon the rights or possessions of another; encroachment; **trespass**." (Emphasis mine).

What are the states to do if the federal government fails to execute their duties to protect the boundaries of American air, land, and water and allows for an invasion? The 10th Amendment of the U.S. Constitution answers that question. It reads,

> "The **powers not delegated** to the United States by the Constitution, nor prohibited by it to the States, **are reserved to the States** respectively, **or** to **the people**." (Emphasis mine).

Simply put, any powers that aren't mentioned in the U.S. Constitution as belonging to the federal government belong to the states themselves and the People of that state. The doctrine of states' rights bars the federal government from interfering with what is *respectively reserved*. In order to prevent the federal government or the states from claiming too much power, the U.S. Constitution's *Supremacy Clause* holds that all laws enacted by the state governments must comply with the constitution and that whenever a law enacted by a state conflicts with a federal law, the federal law must be applied. Aliens entering into any state from a foreign country without processing through the *Uniform Rule of Naturalization* constitutes an *invasion* according to the U.S. Constitution in Article I. Sec. 8, Clause 4. The federal government is constitutionally mandated to intervene and protect all states. It is the *Supremacy Clause* that binds the states to enforce the laws, defend liberty, secure rights, and protect the People wherever the federal government fails to invoke its just authority.

As governor it would be within my vested powers to secure and place a moratorium on California's points of entry utilizing the state's uniformed militia and local municipalities as our federal government has chosen to allow for the invasion. Though the state National Guard and Air National Guard are commanded by the governor, it is a shared command with the president who also has the authority to call them into service during times of war. However, state national guardsmen have a sworn oath to protect and defend the U.S. Constitution which takes priority over foreign wars and allied diplomatic expeditions because their prime directive is the defense of America and the state they reside in. The federal government has zero authority to order a state's National Guard to stand down from enforcing their constitutional powers where they have failed to uphold them. It is a national guardsman's duty to stop an *invasion*, regardless of how trivial or imposing, at all costs.

State and federal government have a primary responsibility to protect their people and are under no constitutional obligation to quarter violent or non-violent invaders irrelevant if they claim to be asylum seekers or refugees. Without processing through the *Uniform Rule of Naturalization*, all are considered enemy trespassers until, if possible, lawfully proven otherwise. If illegal aliens pouring into a state constitutes an *invasion*, then the federal government has insufficient constitutional authority to intervene and prevent any state from protecting their borders.

States have the power to engage in war when "actually invaded, or in such imminent Danger as will not admit delay," according to the U.S. Constitution in Article I. Sec. 10, Clause 3. The states have every right and duty to protect state land, people, and private or public property.

As a governor, my actions to prevent further hostile entrance or intrusion using state militia and local municipalities would be legal, lawful, and most importantly constitutional. The U.S. Supreme Court case **Bary v. United States**, 273 U.S. 128 states,

> "Then a constitution should receive a literal interpretation **in favor of the Citizen**, is especially true, with respect to those provisions which were

designed to safeguard the liberty and **security of the Citizen** in regard to **person** and **property**." (Emphasis mine).

Any state judge who would attempt to place an injunction supporting *open border* measures would be found wanting and in dereliction of their sworn duty. They could be deemed a domestic enemy of the state. Any state or local legislator who expands supportive *open border* measures would also be found wanting and in dereliction of their sworn duty and could be deemed a domestic enemy of the state. A common misconception is that any statute passed by local or state legislators bearing the appearance of law constitutes law. It does not. If any law is not in agreement with the Supreme Law of the Land, it is null and void. The state militia and County Chief Executor's duty obligates anyone within the National Guard, Air National Guard, or Sheriff's department that are aware of such violations to investigate the actions or willful complicity of our political officials. They would need to gather evidence for prosecution, make an arrest, seek an indictment from a De Jure People's Grand Jury and, if obtained, prosecute to the fullest extent by a trial jury, military tribunal, or all of the above.

Now that we have assessed that the states have the right and independent ability to engage in war against an *invasion*, those who are representatives of the People found domestically proliferating the *invasion* engaging in an *otherwise, other unlawful means* can be subject to a military tribunal. Of course, the question must be asked, can military law apply to civilians or elected representatives? **The short answer is that they can be applied when certain circumstances are met.** Those circumstances include the declaration of martial law, coverage

240

of civilians employed by the armed forces, and specific provisions of the law of war otherwise known as the International Humanitarian Law (IHL). There has never been a state who has made a declaration of martial law and this would not be necessary since the states are already under *imminent danger*. The state militia has the authority to run essential branches of the state including the police, courts, legislature, and any lawmaking body. This would allow them to serve arrest warrants and perform trial proceedings for those who are deemed to have committed crimes or activities aimed at undermining the U.S. Constitution and state(s) constitution among a host of other malfeasance. United States Code; Title 18 (U.S.C.) Section 2381 says that

> "whoever, **owing allegiance** to the United States, **levies war** against them or **adheres to their enemies, giving** them **aid** and **comfort within** the **United States** or elsewhere, **is guilty of treason** and shall **suffer death,** or shall be **imprisoned** not less than five years and fined under this title…and shall be incapable of holding any office under the United States." (Emphasis mine).

A governor along with all other servants of the People owes allegiance in favor of the People. They are demanded to secure their borders.

If a governor without fealty to the People is elected, the current status quo may prevail and a continued deterioration of the U.S. Constitution and the People's freedoms will take place. What should the People do if all our lawful efforts fail to stem the tide of corruption and the actions of a reckless government becomes a danger to its own people? What should the People do under absolutism? The answer is simple. All representatives are bound to the oaths they take upon entering their respective positions. They must operate within the confines of the U.S. Constitution and their respective state constitutions. Those vested, just powers are derived only from the *consent of the governed*. We would need to do exactly what our Forefathers told us to do in times of peril. The Declaration of Independence states,

> "...that **whenever any form of government becomes destructive** of these ends, it is **the right of the people to alter or** to **abolish** it, and to institute new government, laying its foundation on such principles, and organizing its powers in such form, as to them shall seem most likely to effect their safety and happiness... But **when a long train of abuses and usurpations**, pursuing invariably the same object, evinces a design to **reduce them under absolute despotism**, it is their right, **it is their duty, to throw off such government, and to provide new guards for their future security.**" (Emphasis mine).

If I construe only the above emphasized, that section of the Declaration of Independence amplifies that the People must be willing to enlist themselves as new guards. A New Guardsman Act would require the People to initiate public debates, forums, engage in intentional discourse in a similar fashion to the process our Founding Fathers partook when determining the best course of action to approach expressing their complaints to the Crown. It was a simplistic and intelligent way to represent all the people of the colonies in first presenting their grievances with the King of Britain and then determining a decisive and united action once their attempt for rectification

242

was rejected. A need to configure horrid proven injuries and tyrannical acts is required by the People to be submitted to a justly movement. Our Founders petitioned 29 redresses of grievances that fell on the King of Britain's deaf ears.

Once again, Americans are subjugated to scandalous governance. The People of America have been making their complaints known before their government and the resolution for those grievances have been ignored by government officials whose oath binds them to serve the Will of the People. The blatant disregard for the Will of the People requires civic public dissertations to discuss the merit of the People's intentions towards abolishment. It is a discussion that is not to be taken lightly nor without careful consideration. All other peaceable efforts should have been exhausted before embarking on this path. If it is determined that there is no other recourse that remains, a unity among the People will be required which can only be obtained through this type of discourse. This would be necessary in order to move forward.

All disquisitions should first be conducted in front of the People's city councils, board of supervisors, legislative state members, the chief executor of their county, and any official's town hall meetings. By addressing the People of their communities present in those sessions directly, while ensuring the presence of the elected representatives, the People would be taking back the power that the U.S. Constitution bestowed upon the *governed* and would remind the elected officials of the limitation to their authority.

Hopefully through the utterances of abolishment, further government decay would be prevented. If it is not, then the People must be prepared to commission legitimate civil unrest by way of armament. Seeking common ground with the corrupt would be futile. For what does a criminal have in common with the upright? An act of abolishment would require the People to engage in their 2nd Amendment right just as America's Forefathers had done. The People would need to mutually pledge their lives to each other and appeal only to the Supreme Judge of the World in a reestablishment of the Declaration of Independence and institute a new government body.

A possible movement towards abolishment of a despotic government is the cardinal reason why America's Founders ensured the 2nd Amendment would never be breached. Maintaining the freedoms expressed in the Declaration of Independence came at a cost to our Forefathers and would also come at a cost again if a reimplementation of the Declaration of Independence became necessary. The People must render a truthful disposition to themselves, do they go quietly into the night under despotic regimes or stand firm on the principals of sovereignty that may incur bloodshed?

No one is coming to save the People of America from itself. If you are unwilling to keep the elected officials accountable to their responsibility to the People and the corruption within government becomes so pervasive that the power of the People is usurped, then you are charged to accept responsibility for the fall of your state and the United States as a whole. Your trepidation and fear or worse your apathy to become involved in your local, state, and federal government will have aided in the proliferation of treachery. You will only have yourself to blame if your rights are stripped away because you did nothing. Our Forefathers understood that maintaining freedoms would never be free from strife.

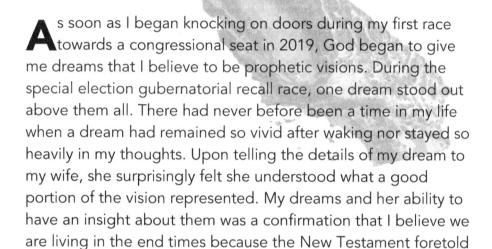

CHAPTER 23

MY CALIFORNIA PROPHECY

As soon as I began knocking on doors during my first race towards a congressional seat in 2019, God began to give me dreams that I believe to be prophetic visions. During the special election gubernatorial recall race, one dream stood out above them all. There had never before been a time in my life when a dream had remained so vivid after waking nor stayed so heavily in my thoughts. Upon telling the details of my dream to my wife, she surprisingly felt she understood what a good portion of the vision represented. My dreams and her ability to have an insight about them was a confirmation that I believe we are living in the end times because the New Testament foretold to us in Joel Chp.2 v.28 (ESV) that

> "And it shall come to pass afterward, that I will
> pour out my Spirit on all flesh; your sons and your
> **daughters shall prophesy,** your old men shall
> **dream dreams, your young men shall see visions."**
> (Emphasis mine).

I feel compelled to share with you the dream that was given to me. Like all dreams and visions blessed by the Holy Spirit it is a gift not to be dismissed and is always to be tested as we read in 1 Thessalonians Chp.5 v.19-22 (NIV) that says,

> "Do not quench the Spirit. Do not treat

245

prophecies with contempt but **test them all**; hold on to what is good, reject every kind of evil." (Emphasis mine).

This dream occurred after I had attended one of my political forums. I drove through the night into the early morning from Sacramento to my home in Ventura County. I felt a level of exhaustion from campaigning that was overwhelming my mind and ached my body. I quickly took a hot shower, laid down to sleep, and before I knew it, I was inside a very lucid and perplexing dream.

The dream began with me sitting in the back seat of a black government SUV. I was being driven down the California Pacific Coast Highway that runs alongside the state's shoreline with three men who were an armed security detail. I was dressed in a professional looking charcoal colored business suit, black shoes, white colored shirt, and grey tie. The men were all dressed in the typical government security detail attire of dark colored suits. The driver appeared to be older in age and rough looking. He was a fair skinned male with dirty blond hair and a light scruff upon his face. The second security man was in the front passenger seat. I sat behind him. He was a black man, clean shaven, and had a high and tight military type haircut. He had a stillness about him that was tense and brawny. The third man to my left was sitting behind the driver. He was the youngest of the three. His skin was brown and he appeared to be Hispanic or of Latin descent. He too was clean shaven, but had slightly unkempt hair compared to the other men. He sat with proper posture almost like he was still earning his keep. These men were not an arresting security detail, but rather they were my protectors.

The drive was quiet with just the hum of the automobile engine and murmur of the traveling wind. I was curious as to who I was that warranted such a rugged security team. It was almost as if I was looking through a different pair of eyes. As I scanned around the inside of the vehicle, I suddenly heard nuclear sirens going off across the PCH. Our cell phones began to vibrate with an alert. The driver quickly turned the radio on to try and catch any immediate news as to why emergency broadcast signals were being sent out. I suddenly felt a deep rumble shifting the ground under the car as the driver picked up speed. While the driver was swiftly banking around cars, the other two men checked their handguns and clips making sure they were locked and loaded. I gazed past the young Hispanic man's window and saw a greyish blue ripple miles out along the horizon. The ripple moved just above the coastal waters that stretched out from left to right beyond what the human eye could see. At first, I thought it was just fog, but as each consecutive moment passed, I realized I was seeing a tidal wave gaining height and rapidly advancing closer to the shore.

Time seemed to have jumped quickly ahead in my dream. I was now outside the vehicle as my security team was trying to hurry me back into the SUV that was now parked on the side of the road. I was screaming and shouting for people to hurry. I remember yelling to the men, "not yet, we need to keep warning the people to hurry, get to higher ground, and get somewhere guarded." The young Hispanic man looked out over the ocean and shouted that we were out of time. I turned. As I looked, I saw a dark blue tidal wave as high as the Empire State Building accelerating toward the shore and a sound like that of roaring lions painfully filled my ears.

The young Hispanic security man told the other two men to get me to safety and that he would take care of the remaining stragglers. The two men took out their weapons and seemed to know where to quickly take me. They both rotated their position around me with one in the front and the other behind as they urged me to start running. We raced towards an oddly shaped twenty or thirty story building just off the highway on a hilltop near other similar buildings. Rather than escort me up to the highest floor, the two men went down into the lower level parking structure. Both men found a maintenance room with double doors locked in the open position in the corner of the structure. They asked that I stand toward the end of the room near the back wall while they stood guard at the immediate opening. The driver looked back at me and said, "Sir, when the water hits the building, it will slowly make its way down to this room. Just before the water touches your face, take in two deep breaths. You'll be fine." Before I knew it, the tidal wave had engulfed the building. There was a muffling thump that overcame the building as if I was in the quietness of space. Both men looked back at me, nodded, and aimed their weapons towards the rush of the water. They both began to shoot the water unloading round after round, clip after clip. I was taken aback by the mere fact that they would even consider shooting a single round at water that could not possibly be stopped by mere bullets.

As the flood rushed toward the double doored entrance and impacted the room, the three of us were suddenly enveloped in an air bubble. The brawny security guard turned back to me and shouted, "Here it comes, Sir! Take your two deep breaths and the water will recede." The bubble started to shrink in tighter with the pulsating movement of a heartbeat. I could hear both men take in their breaths just before they were consumed. It was strange. The water stopped at my face. I looked through it and could still see the two men standing with their guns raised at the ready. I closed my eyes when I saw that the water was beginning to slowly get closer to touching my face and began to gently wrap around my body. I didn't realize until I was under water that I had forgotten to take in my two deep breaths. I felt a mental nudge, a whisper in my mind that said, "Now...take your two slow deep breaths." I thought to myself, "Underwater?" I felt a gentle peace about the instructions and believed I could trust the prompting. I took in my two deep breaths. Somehow, I was able to find the oxygen my body needed despite being submerged in water. It felt like a miracle. When I could feel the desire to take another breath, the water quickly began to recede. As fast as the water had overtaken the land was as swiftly as it returned to its natural resting place.

Time jumped forward once again in my dream and the men and I were now suddenly standing on the top of the building overlooking a devastated California. I could see a few pockets of land with survivors helping others reach the areas that were not nearly as ravaged. I was shocked at the annihilation, but my focus was thankful for those that heeded the warning and survived.

Time seemed to have jumped ahead once more and I found myself standing on lush green terrain near a cliff overlooking a new ocean front. About a hundred yards away near the cliff was a large two-story home that was filled with people. When I walked inside, it appeared that the home belonged to me. I felt I had a familiar connection with the people there even though I didn't really know who they were. I was surrounded by loud conversations of plans being made for community agriculture, protection for children, and proposals for using other homes

249

and lands to train a new tier of soldiers and security forces. A young blonde woman with bright blue eyes smiled at me and pointed out one of the house windows in a building not far off in the distance. Somehow, she knew I was looking for my wife and children.

There was another time jump when I blinked. I was now walking through a media printing press where my wife was leading the charge. Every person I passed by seemed to be in shock that I was alive. Many of them stopped what they were doing to point in the direction my wife was in. When I looked across the work room, there was my wife. She had press ink smeared all over her hands and forehead. Her hair was disheveled and partly tied up in a little ponytail. I could tell she was a little uptight and flustered with handling the day to day, but the second she saw me she ran to me. We quickly embraced and kissed as if we hadn't seen each other for months. After our kiss, I looked at her with tears coming down my face and before I could ask, she answered my question. She said, "The kids are all here and they're fine." After we held each other for a few more moments, I woke up.

When I told my wife about this dream and what I thought it meant, she felt she could help me gain more clarity regarding it. The following is a compilation of both our thoughts on the vision…in part. I say in part because not everything in the dream has been revealed to me.

Let's dive in. The dream begins when I was in a government vehicle and provided with a security detail similar to what many of our representatives are provided today. My understanding is that I was either heavily sought out and thrust into a position by the People of California or the United States that required protection or I was an actual elected servant of the People.

The three security men are either a representation of angels sent to protect me or they are symbolizing people who will be an extra pair of eyes that cover my six during a perilous time. The three men may also represent the primary ethnic backgrounds that dominate the demographic of the state. Their seated positions in the vehicle portray the People's subconscious status of ethnic backgrounds within the culture of California.

The incoming blue tidal wave, we believe, had two meanings. The first interpretation is that the tidal wave represents the Democratic party that is overrunning California. The Democratic party is most often associated with the color blue. Like all tidal waves that grow in size as they get closer to what they might destroy, California is a corrupt supermajority blue state. The Democratic party is growing more and more powerful. The speed at which they legislate will catch many off guard and eventually drown out a good portion of the People's prosperity. Few will survive their onslaught of egregious enactments. The impact their tyranny will have on all Californians will be devastating. Furthermore, by their own evil efforts, they will in-turn bring destruction upon themselves which is one of the reasons why the water recedes so quickly and settles back into a proper resting place. The natural order of California will be reset to where it was always meant to be despite their attempt to overtake it. The second explanation is that there may potentially be an actual tidal wave that will unsuspectingly hit California. The tidal wave may be caused by a massive bomb, weather modification, or an earthquake. Sadly, regardless of which interpretation is correct or whether they both occur simultaneously, California will be in devastation and disarray.

The emergency signal broadcast symbolizes the Watchmen on the wall trying to sound the alarm. I consider myself to also be a Watchman. This explains why I am telling people to hurry and to get to higher ground. I am rushing to help others because I can see the inevitable future that no one else seems to notice

The two remaining security men also carry two possible meanings. The first interpretation is that they are my physical protectors. They signify that I may have guardians who might intervene to safeguard me in a moment of need. The second explanation is that these men who appear to be rough around the edges are various old school veterans that will help in fending off the attack of unscrupulous representatives. This explains why they were shooting at the water. Again, the water may symbolize a sea of Democrats. Because the water engulfs me, it appears the Democrats will continue to thwart the efforts of conservatives attempting to get into office. This will only last a brief time which is why the water swiftly recedes.

The security men took me down to the lower level of the building because that is where I have discovered the corruption is hiding. The knowledge needed to put these degenerates behind bars has been kept away from the People and placed in the lowest levels of public domain where no one would ever think to look. The two guardians help me fight off the barrage. In the end of that battle, we rise above the hidden lies despite the carnage of the state.

The two breaths are a representation of the two gubernatorial elections I will have run in. At first, my wife thought the 2021 California Recall and the 2022 gubernatorial race were symbolizing the two breaths. The failure of the Recall merged right into the 2022 gubernatorial race. This leads me to believe that those races actually only encompass one breath. Therefore, the second breath will be the 2026 gubernatorial election cycle. My wife believes there is another reason behind the two breaths, but this has yet to be revealed to either of us.

When I am standing up on top of the building overlooking a very devastated California, I could see a few remaining pockets of counties and cities that remained functioning like little siloed islands. They had been able to weather the tidal wave. They appeared to be reaching out to the surrounding devastated areas to build bridges and offer support. This possibly represents that a few literal counties and cities in California will have the ability to begin the very long journey of cleaning and fixing up the state, but the primary infrastructure and corrupt government will no longer exist. Somehow, I seem to have played a part in all of that. It has yet to be revealed to my wife and I in what capacity this will be.

Standing on the lush green terrain near a cliff and looking out over a new ocean front indicated to me that I was overlooking a new sea of people. It may also mean that the state of California possibly was no longer recognizable because it will become filled with a new people in the aftermath of the destruction and a refreshed prosperity will be found.

The new home I walked into was potentially a new state capital or headquarters. This would explain why there were so many people, meetings, and discussions about protecting agriculture, children, and providing new military personnel training.

I believe my wife was heading the media because she has always been immensely truthful. In her beautiful honesty, she really doesn't understand why anyone wouldn't just tell the truth. In the dream, she is the representation of a newly led media by everyday people ensuring there are no further lies, deceit, or yellow press. It is an indication that there will be a rise in truthful journalism.

My children are not in the vision because they represent all children who are in danger from the radical democrats legislating laws that are designed to steal children from their parents. My children's safety represents that all the children will be protected by the parents who have had enough of the immorality and exploitation.

These are the revelations given to my wife and I regarding my dream. Not all of the dream has clarity and many aspects of it may hold multiple meanings. We may only understand this in part because all things will be revealed in His timing and it is not for us to know yet. My wife and I pray continuously that His will be done.

CHAPTER 24

FINAL WORDS

I find this chapter to be the most difficult to write. I struggle to find the appropriate words that will inspire you to engage in what is actionable and to fight for what the American people have left of our sovereignty. The word sovereignty is repugnant to the *sons of disobedience* that we now know are the Elite. They are the salacious barons pulling all the strings. They don't believe the People should ever have supreme power or authority over their autocracy because it would eliminate their ability to profit and manipulate the nations of the world. They hate His will and His law written in the hearts of all men. In short, they abhor God, Jesus.

America was always designed to be a free nation, never to be ruled by the Crown or any form of tyrannical regime. The Framers crafted our constitution with such diligence as to ensure the power of right would be vastly difficult to usurp. We must always remember that the consent of the governed gives only one real authority to the servants of the People and that is power to preserve the rights of a free people, granted under the *Laws of Nature and of Nature's God*. Unalienable rights are the liberties endowed by the Creator, not man. No one man can ever truly rule the Earth because it was never theirs to begin with. But like the old song goes, "From the Redwood Forest to the Gulf Stream waters, this land (*and all lands*) were made for you and me." The word *made* is the key word. We

255

were meant to live with the land in order to properly cultivate prosperity with each other. We were not meant to dominate over the inheritance the Earth yields for self-gratification.

Century after century the kingdoms, empires, provinces, and governments of the world have risen and have fallen. Why should America and our current generations experience anything less? If the People fail to recognize the blessings bestowed upon the United States by God, then this young, beautiful, and spectacular nation will fall. Is America, your state, your county, your city, your community worth one more fight to keep this American light shining like a bright beacon on the hill for just a little while longer?

Another saying many of us have heard is *he who dies with the most toys, still dies.* It is greatly overlooked that we are all born into this world with nothing but the flesh we've been given and a soul we must protect from damnation. When we pass away there is no physical material that can come with us into heaven or even hell for that matter.

I struggle with the mere idea of any one person trying to rule over their neighbor. All human life was meant to be shared, not dominated. Celebrated, not weakened. Dignified, not demoralized. Cherished, not exploited. Experienced, not toiled. Lived, not perished. In the end, we are meant to love life, not death.

So, I leave you with one final verse. This one verse keeps me grounded while in pursuit of the California governorship and in pursuit of the hard truths. It is Matthew Chp.20 v.26-28 (NKJV). It reads,

"Yet it shall not be so among you; but whoever desires **to become great** among you, **let him be your servant.** And whoever desires **to be first** among you, **let him be your slave,** just as the **Son of Man** did not come to be served, but **to serve,** and **to give His life** a ransom for many." (Emphasis mine).

Let those who take up the mantle to secure the rights of a free people desire first only to be your servant, just as the Son of Man did.

ACKNOWLEDGMENT

The world is strengthened by those who stand against tyrannical regimes that aim to saturate our peaceful, loving, and God-fearing communities with treachery. To all the individuals who stood by me during my campaigns and continue to stand by my message, I want to say thank you. It was your prayers, support, and countless hours of research and outreach that helped make the writing of this book possible.

To my Campaign Manager, Treasurer, and sister, Elena, thank you for the endless hours you spent traveling, planning, researching, and praying over me during every event. It allowed me to discover the hard truths that obscure the People from living in prosperity. Your steadfastness during the hardships of our political adventures is something I will forever be grateful for and cherish.

To my brother in Christ, Eric, one the most humble and intelligent men I've ever come across. You were and remain an incredible inspiration as I have witnessed you fighting the good fight first hand and endure insurmountable attacks upon your family and livelihood that the average person would have succumbed to. Your investigative skills encouraged me to dig deeper and break through the lies. We remain brothers in this battle until Jesus returns.

The grievances and information regarding the overwhelming deceit I learned about that plagues our nation and state exhausted me. It was because I was blessed with amazing team members and friends who shared my beliefs, helped lightened the burden, and cheered me forward that I was able to continue on. To Justin, J Marie, Alexis, Karen, and Joe, you have my deepest gratitude.

Without a platform to share all that I have discovered and learn from other truthers who are equally in the trenches, the battle fought alone to break free of our shackles can weaken even the strongest of us. It is with heartfelt and a spirited appreciation that I am extremely thankful to Pastor Raul, Hope, Andrew and Light Dove Ministries, Pastor Ron, Jeremy, Judy and the toughest freedom fighter I know Patriots for Freedom's Sonya. You are warriors for Christ and I am proud to be by your side.

To my mother Liz, my brother Frank, my sisters Dee, Karla, and Carmela, my Aunt Suzanna and Uncle Steve, my father-in-law Richard and mother-in-law Kathy, I thank you for your continued backing, honesty, and shared excitement and support throughout my candidacies.

Having an idea and turning it into a book is as hard as it sounds, but I could not have completed this book without my wife, Melissa. From reading early drafts to giving me advice on the cover design of my book, thank you. I love you forever!

Finally, to my father. Even though my father was plagued by alcoholism, he planted the seed of Jesus deeply in me. The root of my belief and faith in Christ are unshaken and unwavering to this very day, thanks to my father. Sadly, many years ago, my father was diagnosed with cancer. He went into remission for nearly two years before he passed away, clear minded and free from the stronghold of alcohol. I felt fortunate to have been able to spend quality time with him when he was sober, happy, and fun. He would share humorous stories and was great to laugh with. I was the only one among my siblings who loved playing chess and discussing end times prophecy with him. The book of Revelation was our thing. I forgave him for the many years of abuse long before he was diagnosed with cancer. I felt blessed to have reconciled our relationship. His passing was bittersweet. The conversations my father and I had about how the book of Revelation would begin to unravel are now unfolding before this generation's eyes. There was a certain pull I felt on my spirit, a sort of passing of the baton from my father to me, pushing me to continue to be a Watchman on the wall sounding the alarm. For that I am humbled, privileged, and eternally honored.

RESOURCES

I have, to the best of my ability, provided a list of the resources that were key to my research. My hope is that this book will assist you on your own journey to finding the Truth.

RELIGIOUS RESOURCES

I.	The Holy Bible
II.	The Book of Jubilees
III.	The Qur'an
IV.	Islamic Caliphates World History Encyclopedia

CONSTITUTIONAL RESOURCES

V.	Declaration of Independence
VI.	The United States Constitution
VII.	The California State Constitution (2023)
VIII.	Federalist Papers
IX.	Debates of the Federal Convention (1787)
X.	Letter to John Taylor (1814)

JUDICIAL RESOURCES

XI.	Marbury v. Madison (1803), 5 U.S. 137
XII.	Hoke v. Henderson (1839), 38 U.S. 230
XIII.	Yick Wo v. Hopkins (1886), 118 U.S. 356
XIV.	Coffin v. Ogden (1873), 85 U.S. 120, 124 (Maxim of Law: 15d.)
XV.	Butchers Union v. Crescent City Co. (1884), 111 U.S. 746
XVI.	Murdock v. Pennsylvania (1943), 319 U.S. 105
XVII.	Wieman v. Updegraff (1952), 344 U.S. 183
XVIII.	United States v. Minker (1956), 350 U.S. 179
XIX.	Miranda v. Arizona (1966), 384 U.S. 436

XX.   Vogel v. County of Los Angeles (1967), 68 Cal. 2d 18
XXI.   Shuttleworth v. City of Birmingham Alabaman (1968), 394 U.S. 147
XXII.   United States v. Williams (1992), 112 S.Ct. 1735, 504 U.S. 36, 118 L.Ed.2d 352
XXIII. Jesson v. Davis (2002), 97 Cal. App. 4th 1032
XXIV.   Association for Molecular Pathology v. Myriad Genetics (2013), 569 U.S. 576

LAW RESOURCES

XXV.   Black's Law Dictionary 11th Edition
XXVI.   American Jurisprudence - 16Am Jur 2d, Sec. 98
XXVII. Corpus Juris Secundum Volume 7, Sec. 5: Attorney & Client Relationship

FEDERAL and STATE CODE(S) RESOURCES

XXVIII. United States Code; Title 28 (U.S.C.) Section 3002 – Subsection 15 & 15A
XXIX.   United States Code; Title 18 (U.S.C.) Section 2381
XXX.   United States Code; Title 18 (U.S.C.) Section 2384
XXXI.   California Government Code Section 1368
XXXII. California Government Code Section 1369
XXXIII. California Government Code Section 3108
XXXIV. California Government Code Section 3109
XXXV.   California Penal Code Section 1170 Subdivision (h)
XXXVI. American Presidency Project: Executive Order 14067: Ensuring Responsibility Development of Digital Assets. Sec. 4 (a) (iii)

ARTICLE RESOURCES

XXXVII. Newstarget.com, February 9, 2022
XXXVIII. Todayonline.com, October 11, 2021
XXXIX.   French Hill News, November 20, 2019
XL.   Marketscreener.com, September 22, 2021
XLI.   Federal Reserve Inaugural Conference, June 6, 2022
XLII.   Insider News, March 2, 2023
XLIII.   NIH National Library of Medicine and National Center for Biotechnology Information, September 29, 2021
XLIV.   ABC News, September 13, 2023
XLV.   Opendemocracy.net, August 24, 2021
XLVI.   Rangefire.us, April 25, 2022
XLVII.   Fox News Economist, October 19, 2022
XLVIII. USA Today, April 30, 2023
XLIX.   EWG.org, May 22, 2022
L.   News18.com, February 18, 2021

LI.   ABC 23 News, January 13, 2023
LII.   The Smithsonian Magazine, July 14, 2022
LIII. Global Salmon Initiative
LIV.   Family Friendly Farms
LV.   The Stew Peters Show, 2021

STATE AGENCY REPORT RESOURCES

LVI.   National Interagency Fire Center 2023 Report
LVII.   Federal Railroad Administration 2022 Report
LVIII. Energy Information Administration (EIA) 2022 Report
LIX.   World Deaths Statistics 2022 Report
LX.   World Health Organization 2023 Report
LXI.   K-12 School Shooting Database 2022-2023 Report

MISCELLANEOUS RESOURCES

LXII.   The American Heritage Dictionary of the English Language, 5th Edition
LXIII. Merriam Webster Dictionary
LXIV.   Cambridge Oxford Dictionary

DISCLAIMER

FAIR USE COPYRIGHT NOTICE

Made in the USA
Columbia, SC
30 July 2024

39188583R00147